THE O'LEARY SERIES

Microsoft® PowerPoint® 2000
Brief Version

Timothy J. O'Leary
Arizona State University

Linda I. O'Leary

Boston   Burr Ridge, IL   Dubuque, IA   Madison, WI   New York
San Francisco   St. Louis   Bangkok   Bogotá   Caracas   Lisbon
London   Madrid   Mexico City   Milan   New Delhi   Seoul
Singapore   Sydney   Taipei   Toronto

McGraw-Hill Higher Education

A Division of The McGraw-Hill Companies

4 5 6 7 8 9 0 BAN/BAN 9 0 9 8 7 6 5 4 3 2 1 0

ISBN 0-07-233752-4

Vice president/Editor-in-chief: *Michael W. Junior*
Publisher: *David Brake*
Sponsoring editor: *Trisha O'Shea*
Developmental editor: *Stephen Fahringer*
Senior marketing manager: *Jodi McPherson*
Senior project manager: *Beth Cigler*
Manager, new book production: *Melonie Salvati*
Freelance design coordinator: *Gino Cieslik*
Cover design: *Francis Owens*
Supplement coordinator: *Marc Mattson*
Compositor: *Rogondino & Associates*
Typeface: *11/13 Century Book*
Printer: *The Banta Book Group*

Library of Congress Catalog Card Number 99-62023

http://www.mhhe.com

THE O'LEARY SERIES

Microsoft® PowerPoint® 2000

Brief Version

Timothy J. O'Leary
Arizona State University

Linda I. O'Leary

Boston   Burr Ridge, IL   Dubuque, IA   Madison, WI   New York
San Francisco   St. Louis   Bangkok   Bogotá   Caracas   Lisbon
London   Madrid   Mexico City   Milan   New Delhi   Seoul
Singapore   Sydney   Taipei   Toronto

At McGraw-Hill Higher Education, we publish instructional materials targeted at the higher education market. In an effort to expand the tools of higher learning, we publish texts, lab manuals, study guides, testing materials, software, and multimedia products.

At **Irwin/McGraw-Hill** (a division of McGraw-Hill Higher Education), we realize that technology has created and will continue to create new mediums for professors and students to use in managing resources and communicating information with one another. We strive to provide the most flexible and complete teaching and learning tools available as well as offer solutions to the changing world of teaching and learning.

Irwin/McGraw-Hill **is dedicated to providing the tools for today's instructors and students to successfully navigate the world of Information Technology.**

■ **Seminar series**—Irwin/McGraw-Hill's Technology Connection seminar series offered across the country every year demonstrates the latest technology products and encourages collaboration among teaching professionals.

■ **Osborne/McGraw-Hill**—This division of The McGraw-Hill Companies is known for its best-selling Internet titles *Harley Hahn's Internet & Web Yellow Pages* and the *Internet Complete Reference*. Osborne offers an additional resource for certification and has strategic publishing relationships with corporations such as Corel Corporation and America Online. For more information visit Osborne at **www.osborne.com**.

■ **Digital solutions**—Irwin/McGraw-Hill is committed to publishing digital solutions. Taking your course online doesn't have to be a solitary venture, nor does it have to be a difficult one. We offer several solutions that will allow you to enjoy all the benefits of having course material online. For more information visit **www.mhhe.com/solutions/index.mhtml**.

■ **Packaging options**—For more about our discount options, contact your local Irwin/McGraw-Hill Sales representative at 1-800-338-3987 or visit our Web site at **www.mhhe.com/it**.

Preface

Goals/Philosophy

The goal of *The O'Leary Series* is to give students a basic understanding of computing concepts and to build the skills necessary to ensure that information technology is an advantage in whatever path they choose in life. Because we believe that students learn better and retain more information when concepts are reinforced visually, we feature a unique visual orientation coupled with our trademark "learn by doing" approach.

Approach

The O'Leary Series is the true *step-by-step way to develop computer application skills*. The new Microsoft Office 2000 design emphasizes, the step-by-step instructions with full screen captures that illustrate the results of each step performed. Each Tutorial (chapter) follows the "learn by doing" approach in combining conceptual coverage with detailed, software-specific instructions. A running case study that is featured in each tutorial highlights the real-world capabilities of each of the software applications and leads students step by step from problem to solution.

About the Book

The O'Leary Series offers 2 *levels* of instruction: Brief and Introductory. Each level builds upon the previous level.

- **Brief**—This level covers the basics of an application and contains two to three chapters.

- **Introductory**—This level includes the material in the Brief textbook plus two to three additional chapters. The Introductory text prepares students for the *Microsoft Office User Specialist Exam (MOUS Certification)*.

Each tutorial features:

- **Common Office 2000 Features**—This section provides a review of several basic procedures and Windows features. Students will also learn about many of the features that are common to all Microsoft Office 2000 applications.

- **Overview**—The Overview contains a "Before You Begin" section which presents both students and professors with all the information they need to know before starting the tutorials, including hardware and software settings. The Overview appears at the beginning of each lab manual and describes (1) what the program is,

(2) what the program can do, (3) generic terms the program uses, and (4) the Case Study to be presented.

- **Working Together sections**—These sections provide the same hands-on visual approach found in the tutorials to the integration and new collaboration features of Office 2000.

- **Glossary**—The Glossary appears at the end of each text and defines all key terms that appear in boldface type throughout the tutorials and in the end-of-tutorial Key Terms lists.

- **Index**—The Index appears at the end of each text and provides a quick reference to find specific concepts or terms in the text.

Brief Version

The Brief Version is divided into two tutorials, followed by Working Together, which shows the intregration of PowerPoint 2000, Word 2000, and Excel 2000.

Tutorial 1: You will use PowerPoint to enter and edit the text for your presentation. You also learn how to reorganize the presentation and enhance it with different text attributes and by adding a picture and clip art. Finally, you learn how to run a slide show and print handouts.

Tutorial 2: You will learn about many more features to enhance the appearance of your slides. This includes changing the slide design and color scheme and adding animation and sound. You will also learn how to add transitional and build effects to make the presentation more interesting. Finally, you create speaker notes to help you keep your cool during the presentation.

Working Together: This tutorial demonstrates the sharing of information between applications. First you will learn how to copy a table created in Word into a slide. Then you will learn how to link a chart created in Excel to another slide.

Each tutorial features:

- **Step-by-step instructions**—Each tutorial consists of step-by-step instructions along with accompanying screen captures. The screen captures represent how the student's screen should appear after completing a specific step.

- **Competencies**—Listed at the beginning of each tutorial, the Competencies describe what skills will be mastered upon completion of the tutorial.

- **Concept Overview**—Located at the start of each tutorial, the Concept Overviews provide a brief introduction to the concepts to be presented.

- **Concept boxes**—Tied into the Concept Overviews, the Concept boxes appear throughout the tutorial and provide clear, concise explanations of the concepts under discussion, which makes them a valuable study aid.

- **Marginal notes**–Appearing throughout the tutorial, marginal notes provide helpful hints, suggestions, troubleshooting advice, and alternative methods of completing tasks.

- **Case study**–The running case study is carried throughout each tutorial and is based on real use of software in a business setting.

- **End-of-tutorial material**–At the end of each tutorial the following is provided:

   Concept Summary–This two-page spread presents a visual summary of the concepts presented in the tutorial and can be used as a study aid for students.

   Key Terms–This page-referenced list is a useful study aid for students.

   Matching/Multiple Choice/True False Questions

   Command Summary–The Command Summary includes keyboard and toolbar shortcuts.

   Screen Identifications–These exercises ask students to demonstrate their understanding of the applications by identifying screen features.

   Discussion Questions–These questions are designed to stimulate in-class discussion.

   Hands-On Practice Exercises–These detailed exercises of increasing difficulty ask students to create Office documents based on the skills learned in the tutorial.

   On Your Own–These problems of increasing difficulty ask students to employ more creativity and independence in creating Office documents based on new case scenarios.

Acknowledgments

The new edition of the Microsoft Office 2000 has been made possible only through the enthusiasm and dedication of a great team of people. Because the team spans the country, literally from coast to coast, we have utilized every means of working together including conference calls, FAX, e-mail, and document collaboration . . . we have truly tested the team approach and it works!

Leading the team from Irwin/McGraw-Hill are Kyle Lewis, Senior Sponsoring Editor, Trisha O'Shea, Sponsoring Editor, and Steve Fahringer, Developmental Editor. Their renewed commitment, direction, and support have infused the team with the excitement of a new project.

The production staff is headed by Beth Cigler, Senior Project Manager, whose planning and attention to detail has made it possible for us to successfully meet a very challenging schedule. Members of the production team include. Gino Cieslik and Francis Owens, art and design; Pat Rogondino, layout; Susan Defosset and Joan Paterson, copy editing. While all have contributed immensely, I would particularly like to thank Pat and Susan . . . team members for many past editions whom I can always depend on to do a great job. My thanks also go to the project Marketing Manager, Jodi McPherson, for her enthusiastic promotion of this edition.

Finally, I am particularly grateful to a small but very dedicated group of people who helped me develop the manuscript. My deepest appreciation is to my co-author, consultant, and lifelong partner, Tim, for his help and support while I have been working on this edition. Colleen Hayes who has been assisting me from the beginning, continues to be my right arm, taking on more responsibility with each edition. Susan Demar and Carol Dean have also helped on the last several editions and continue to provide excellent developmental and technical support. New to the project this year are Bill Barth, Kathi Duggan, and Steve Willis, who have provided technical expertise and youthful perspective.

Reviewers

We would also like to thank the reviewers for their insightful input and criticism. Their feedback has helped to make this edition even stronger.

Josephine A. Braneky, *New York City Technical College*
Robert Breshears, *Maryville University*

Gary Buterbaugh, *Indiana University of Pennsylvania*
Mitchell M. Charkiewicz, *Bay Path College*
Seth Hock, *Columbus State Community College*
Katherine S. Hoppe, *Wake Forest University*
Lisa Miller, *University of Central Oklahoma*
Anne Nelson, *High Point University*
Judy Tate, *Tarrant County Junior College*
Dottie Sunio, *Leeward Community College*
Charles Walker, *Harding University*
Mark E. Workman, *Blinn College*

Additionally, each semester I hear from students at Arizona State University who are enrolled in the Introduction to Computers course. They constantly provide great feedback from a student's perspective . . . I thank you all.

POWERPOINT 2000

Concept Boxes identify the most important concepts in each Tutorial.

Concept 5 Automatic Grammar Check

The automatic grammar-checking feature advises you of incorrect grammar as you create and edit a document, and proposes possible corrections. If Word detects grammatical errors in subject-verb agreements, verb forms, capitalization, or commonly confused words, to name a few, they are identified with a wavy green line. You can correct the grammatical error by editing it or you can display a suggested correction. Not all grammatical errors identified by Word are actual errors. Use discretion when correcting the errors. Grammar checking does not occur until after you enter punctuation or end a line.

2 ■ Right-click on Announcing four to display the Grammar shortcut menu.

Your screen should be similar to Figure 1–10.

Tables provide quick summaries of toolbar buttons, key terms, and procedures for specific tasks.

Yellow **Additional Information** boxes appear throughout each tutorial and explain additional uses of the application or of a specific topic.

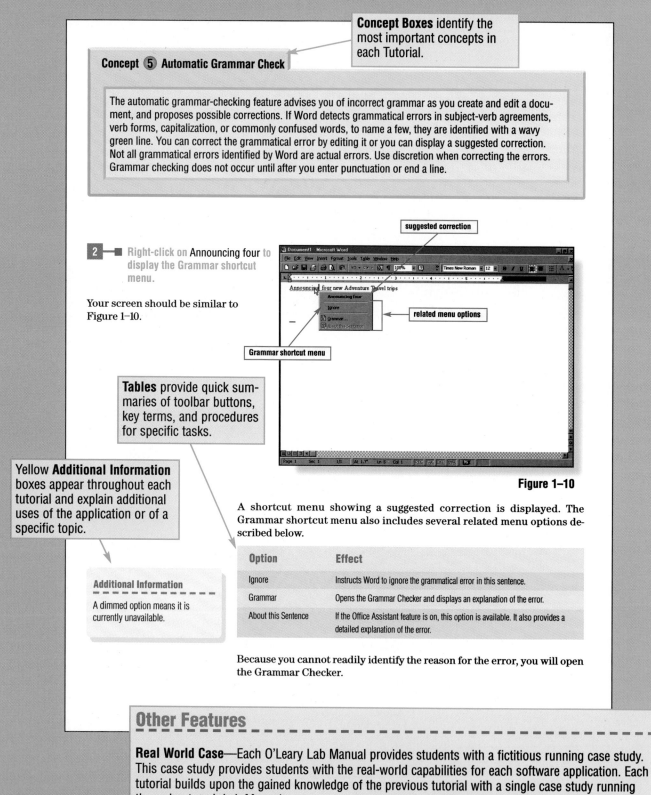

suggested correction

related menu options

Grammar shortcut menu

Figure 1–10

A shortcut menu showing a suggested correction is displayed. The Grammar shortcut menu also includes several related menu options described below.

Additional Information

A dimmed option means it is currently unavailable.

Option	Effect
Ignore	Instructs Word to ignore the grammatical error in this sentence.
Grammar	Opens the Grammar Checker and displays an explanation of the error.
About this Sentence	If the Office Assistant feature is on, this option is available. It also provides a detailed explanation of the error.

Because you cannot readily identify the reason for the error, you will open the Grammar Checker.

Other Features

Real World Case—Each O'Leary Lab Manual provides students with a fictitious running case study. This case study provides students with the real-world capabilities for each software application. Each tutorial builds upon the gained knowledge of the previous tutorial with a single case study running throughout each Lab Manual.

End-of-Chapter Material—Each Tutorial ends with a visual **Concept Summary**. This two-page spread presents a concept summary of the concepts presented in the tutorial and can be used as a study aid for

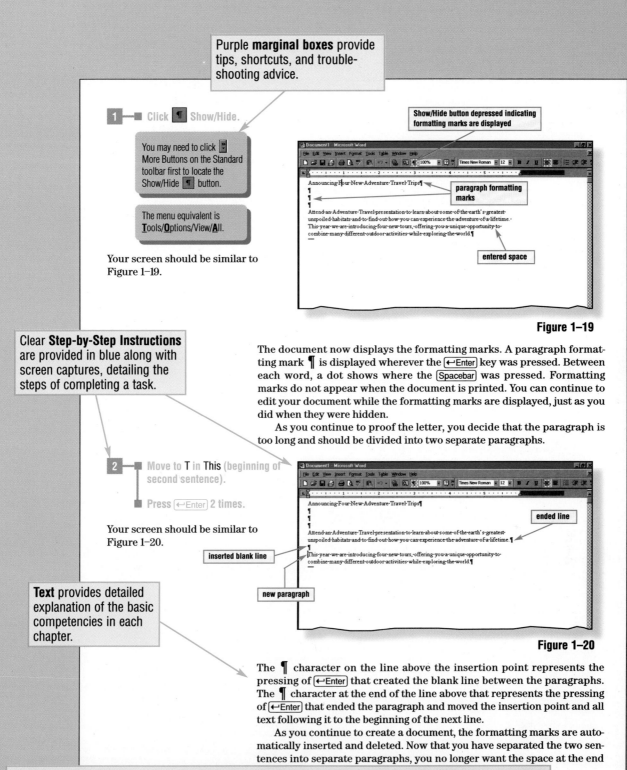

Purple **marginal boxes** provide tips, shortcuts, and trouble-shooting advice.

Clear **Step-by-Step Instructions** are provided in blue along with screen captures, detailing the steps of completing a task.

Text provides detailed explanation of the basic competencies in each chapter.

1 ■ Click ¶ Show/Hide.

You may need to click More Buttons on the Standard toolbar first to locate the Show/Hide ¶ button.

The menu equivalent is **T**ools/**O**ptions/View/**A**ll.

Your screen should be similar to Figure 1–19.

Show/Hide button depressed indicating formatting marks are displayed

paragraph formatting marks

entered space

Figure 1–19

The document now displays the formatting marks. A paragraph formatting mark ¶ is displayed wherever the ⏎Enter key was pressed. Between each word, a dot shows where the Spacebar was pressed. Formatting marks do not appear when the document is printed. You can continue to edit your document while the formatting marks are displayed, just as you did when they were hidden.

As you continue to proof the letter, you decide that the paragraph is too long and should be divided into two separate paragraphs.

2 ■ Move to T in This (beginning of second sentence).

■ Press ⏎Enter 2 times.

Your screen should be similar to Figure 1–20.

inserted blank line

new paragraph

ended line

Figure 1–20

The ¶ character on the line above the insertion point represents the pressing of ⏎Enter that created the blank line between the paragraphs. The ¶ character at the end of the line above that represents the pressing of ⏎Enter that ended the paragraph and moved the insertion point and all text following it to the beginning of the next line.

As you continue to create a document, the formatting marks are automatically inserted and deleted. Now that you have separated the two sentences into separate paragraphs, you no longer want the space at the end

students. A **Key Terms** section and a **Command Summary** table follow the Concept Summary, providing a list of page-referenced terms and keyboard and toolbar shortcuts which can be a useful study aid for students. **Screen Identification**, **Matching**, **Multiple Choice**, and **True False Questions** provide additional reinforcement to the Tutorial Material. **Discussion Questions**, **Hands-on Practice Exercises**, and **On Your Own Exercises** develop critical thinking skills and offer step-by-step practice. These exercises have a rating system from Easy to Difficult and test the student's ability to apply the knowledge they have gained in each tutorial. Each O'Leary Lab Manual provides at least two **On the Web** exercises where students are asked to use the Web to solve a particular problem.

Teaching Resources

The following is a list of supplemental material that can be used to help teach this course.

Active Testing and Learning Assessment Software (ATLAS)

Available for The O'Leary Series is our cutting edge "Real Time Assessment" ATLAS software. ATLAS is web enabled and allows students to perform timed tasks while working live in an application. ATLAS will track how a specific task is completed and the time it takes to complete that task and so measures both proficiency and efficiency. ATLAS will provide full customization and authoring capabilities for professors and can include content from any of our application series.

Instructor's Resource Kits

Instructor's Resource Kits provide professors with all of the ancillary material needed to teach a course. Irwin/McGraw-Hill is committed to providing instructors with the most effective instructional resources available. Many of these resources are available at our Information Technology Supersite, found at **www.mhhe.com/it**. Our Instructor's Resource Kits are available on CD-ROM and contain the following:

- **Diploma by Brownstone**—Diploma is the most flexible, powerful, and easy to use computerized testing system available in higher education. The Diploma system allows professors to create an exam as a printed version, as a LAN-based Online version, or as an Internet version. Diploma also includes grade book features, which automate the entire testing process.

- **Instructor's Manual**—The Instructor's Manual includes solutions to all lessons and end of the unit material, teaching tips and strategies, and additional exercises.

- **Student Data Files**—Students must have student data files in order to complete practice and test sessions. The instructor and students using this text in classes are granted the right to post student data files on any network or stand-alone computer, or to distribute the files on individual diskettes. The student data files may be downloaded from our IT Supersite at **www.mhhe.com/it**

- **Series Web site**—Available at **www.mhhe.com/cit/oleary**.

Digital Solutions

- **Pageout Lite**–This software is designed for you if you're just beginning to explore Web site options. Pageout Lite will help you to easily post your own material online. You may choose one of three templates, type in your material, and PageOut Lite will instantly convert it to HTML.

- **Pageout**–Pageout is our Course Web Site Development Center. Pageout offers a syllabus page, Web site address, Online Learning Center content, online exercises and quizzes, gradebook, discussion board, an area for students to build their own Web pages, plus all features of Pageout Lite. For more information please visit the Pageout Web site at **www.mhla.net/pageout**.

- **OLC/Series Web Sites**–Online Learning Centers (OLCs)/series sites are accessible through our Supersite at **www.mhhe.com/it**. Our Online Learning Centers/series sites provide pedagogical features and supplements for our titles online. Students can point and click their way to key terms, learning objectives, chapter overviews, PowerPoint slides, exercises, and Web links.

- **The McGraw-Hill Learning Architecture (MHLA)**–MHLA is a complete course delivery system. MHLA gives professors ownership in the way digital content is presented to the class through online quizzing, student collaboration, course administration, and content management. For a walk-through of MHLA, visit the MHLA Web Site at **www.mhla.net**.

Packaging Options

For more about our discount options, contact your local Irwin/McGraw-Hill sales representative at 1-800-338-3987 or visit our Web site at **www.mhhe.com/it**.

Contents

Introducing Common Office 2000 Features

This section will review several basic procedures and Windows features. In addition you will learn about many of the features that are common to all Microsoft Office 2000 applications. Although PowerPoint 2000 will be used to demonstrate how the features work, only common features will be addressed. The features that are specific to the application itself will be introduced individually in each tutorial.

Turning on the computer

If necessary, follow the procedure below to turn on your computer.

> Do not have any disks in the drives when you start the computer.

1 ■ **Turn on the power switch.** The power switch is commonly located on the back or right side of your computer. It may also be a button that you push on the front of your computer.

■ **If necessary, turn your monitor on and adjust the contrast and brightness.** Generally, the button to turn on the monitor is located on the front of the monitor. Use the dials (generally located in the panel on the front of the monitor) to adjust the monitor.

> Press [Tab ⇆] to move to the next box.

■ **If you are on a network, you may be asked to enter your User Name and Password. Type the required information in the boxes. When you are done, press** [← Enter].

The Windows program is loaded into the main memory of your computer and the Windows desktop is displayed.

Your screen should be similar to Figure 1.

Figure 1

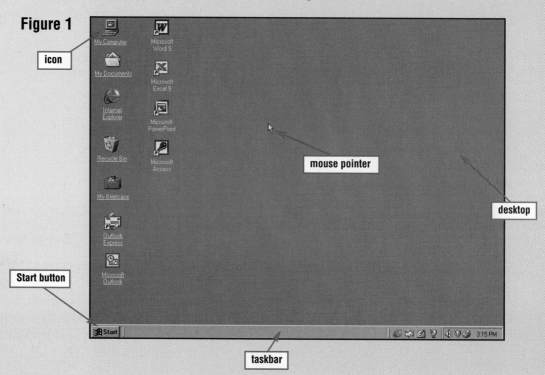

The **desktop** is the opening screen for Windows and is the place where you begin your work using the computer. Figure 1 shows the Windows 98 desktop. If you are using Windows 95 your screen will look slightly different. Small pictures, called **icons**, represent the objects on the desktop. Your desktop will probably display many different icons than shown here. At the bottom of the desktop screen is the **taskbar**. It contains buttons that are used to access programs and features. The **Start button** on the left end of the bar is used to start a program, open a document, get help, find information, and change system settings.

> If a Welcome box is displayed, click ⊠ (in the upper right corner of the box) to close it.

Using a Mouse

> If you are already familiar with using a mouse, skip to the secrtion Loading an Office Application.

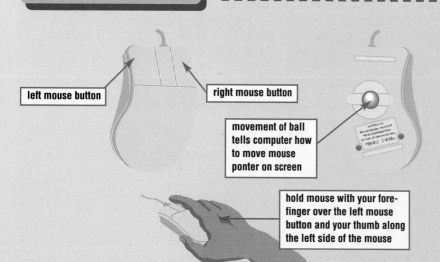

The arrow-shaped symbol on your screen is the **mouse pointer**. It is used to interact with objects on the screen and is controlled by the hardware device called a **mouse** that is attached to your computer.

The mouse pointer changes shape on the screen depending on what it is pointing to. Some of the most common shapes are shown in the table below.

Pointer Shape	Meaning
⌖	Normal select
👆	Link select
⌛	Busy
🚫	Area is not available

On top of the mouse are two or three buttons that are used to choose items on the screen. The mouse actions and descriptions are shown in the table below.

If your system has a stick, ball or touch pad, the buttons are located adjacent to the device.

Action	Description
Point	Move the mouse so the mouse pointer is positioned on the item you want to use.
Click	Press and release a mouse button. The left mouse button is the primary button that is used for most tasks.
Double-click	Quickly press and release the left mouse button twice.
Drag	Move the mouse while holding down a mouse button.

Throughout the labs, "click" means to use the left mouse button. If the right mouse button is to be used, the directions will tell you to right-click on the item.

1 ■ Move the mouse in all directions (up, down, left, and right) and note the movement of the mouse pointer.

■ Point to the 🖥 My Computer icon.

Your screen should be similar to Figure 2.

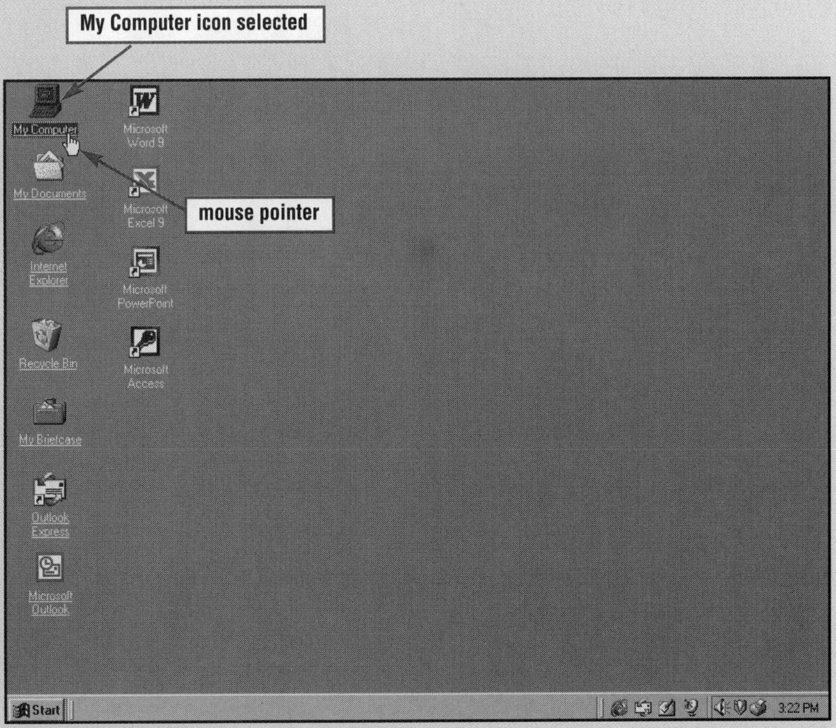

My Computer icon selected

mouse pointer

Figure 2

> Depending on the version of Windows you are using and the setup, the mouse pointer may be ⇧ and you will need to click on the icon to select it.

The pointer on the screen moved in the direction you moved the mouse and currently appears as a ⇧. The icon appears highlighted, indicating it is the selected item and ready to be used. A **ScreenTip** box containing a brief description of the item you are pointing to may be displayed.

Loading an Office Application

There are several ways to start an Office application. One is to use the Start/New Office Document command and select the type of document you want to create. Another is to use Start/Documents and select the document name from the list of recently used documents. This starts the associated application and opens the selected document at the same time. The two most common ways to start an Office 2000 application are by choosing the application name from the Start menu or by clicking a desktop shortcut for the program if it is available.

> Point to a Start menu option to select it; click it to choose it.

1 ■ Click **Start** to display the Start menu.

■ Select **Programs**

■ Choose **Microsoft PowerPoint**.

or

> If you are using Windows 98, depending on your setup, you may only need to single-click the shortcut.

■ Double click the **Shortcut to Powerpnt.exe** shortcut.

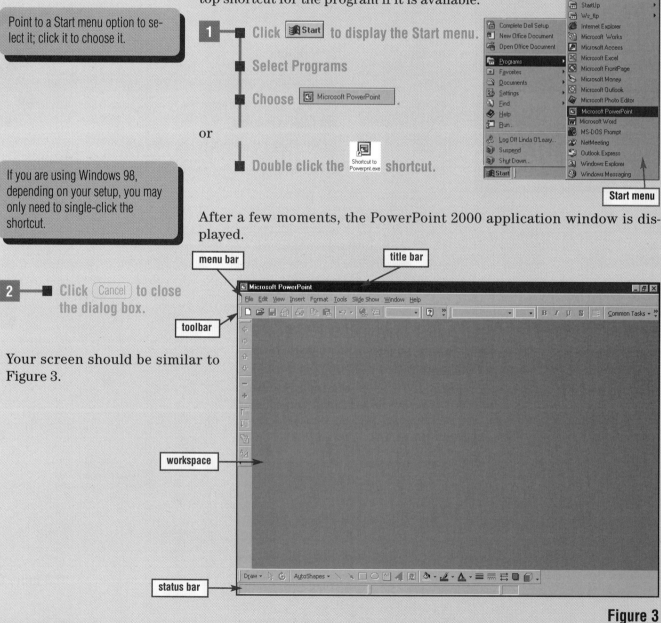

After a few moments, the PowerPoint 2000 application window is displayed.

2 ■ Click **Cancel** to close the dialog box.

Your screen should be similar to Figure 3.

Figure 3

Basic Windows Features

As you can see, many of the features in the PowerPoint window are the same as in other Windows applications. Among those features is a title bar, a menu bar, toolbars, a document window, scroll bars, and mouse compatibility. You can move and size Office application windows, select commands, use Help, and switch between files and programs, just as you can in Windows. The common user interface makes learning and using new applications much easier.

TITLE BAR

The PowerPoint window **title bar** displays the program name, Microsoft PowerPoint. The left end of the title bar contains the PowerPoint application window ⬛ Control-menu icon, and the right end displays the ⬛ Minimize, ⬛ Restore, and ⬛ Close buttons. They perform the same functions and operate in the same way as in Windows 95 and Windows 98.

1— ■ If necessary, click ⬜ in the title bar to maximize the application window.

MENU BAR

The **menu bar** below the title bar displays the PowerPoint program menu, which consists of nine menus. As you use the Office applications you will see that the menu bar contains many of the same menus, such as File, Edit and Help. You will also see several menus that are specific to each application. You will learn about using the menus in the next section.

TOOLBARS

The **toolbar** located below the menu bar contains, buttons that are mouse shortcuts for many of the menu items. Commonly, the Office applications will display two toolbars when the application is first opened; Standard and Formatting. They may appear together on one row or on separate rows. You will learn about using the toolbars shortly.

WORKSPACE

The **workspace** is the large center area of the PowerPoint application window where presentations are displayed in open windows. Multiple presentations can be open and displayed in the workspace at the same time.

STATUS BAR

The **status bar** at the bottom of the window displays location information and the status of different settings as they are used. Different information is displayed in the status bar for different applications.

Using Office 2000 Features

- -

MENUS

A **menu** is one of many methods you can use to tell a program what you want it to do. When opened, a menu displays a list of commands. Most menus appear in a menu bar. Other menus pop up when you right-click (click the right mouse button) on an item. This type of menu is called a **shortcut menu**.

1 ■ Click File to open the File menu.

Your screen should be similar to Figure 4.

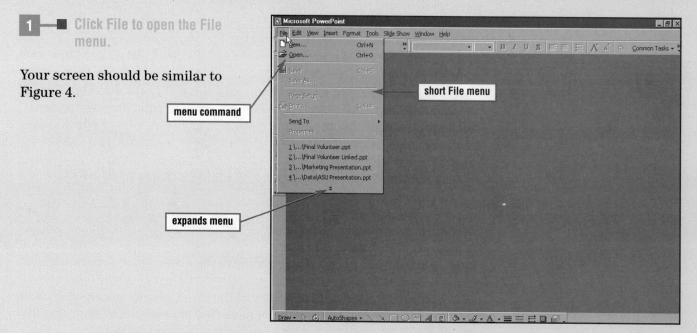

menu command

short File menu

expands menu

Figure 4

When a menu is first opened, it displays a short version of commands. The short menu displays basic commands when the application is first used. As you use the application, those commands you use frequently are listed on the short menu and others are hidden. Because the short menu is personalized automatically to the user's needs, different commands may be listed on your file menu than appear in Figure 4 above.

An expanded version will display automatically after the menu is opened for a few seconds (see Figure 5). If you do not want to wait for the expanded version to appear, you can click ▾ at the bottom of the menu and the menu list expands to display all commands.

> You can double-click the menu name to show the expanded menu immediately.

Your screen should be similar to Figure 5.

Figure 5

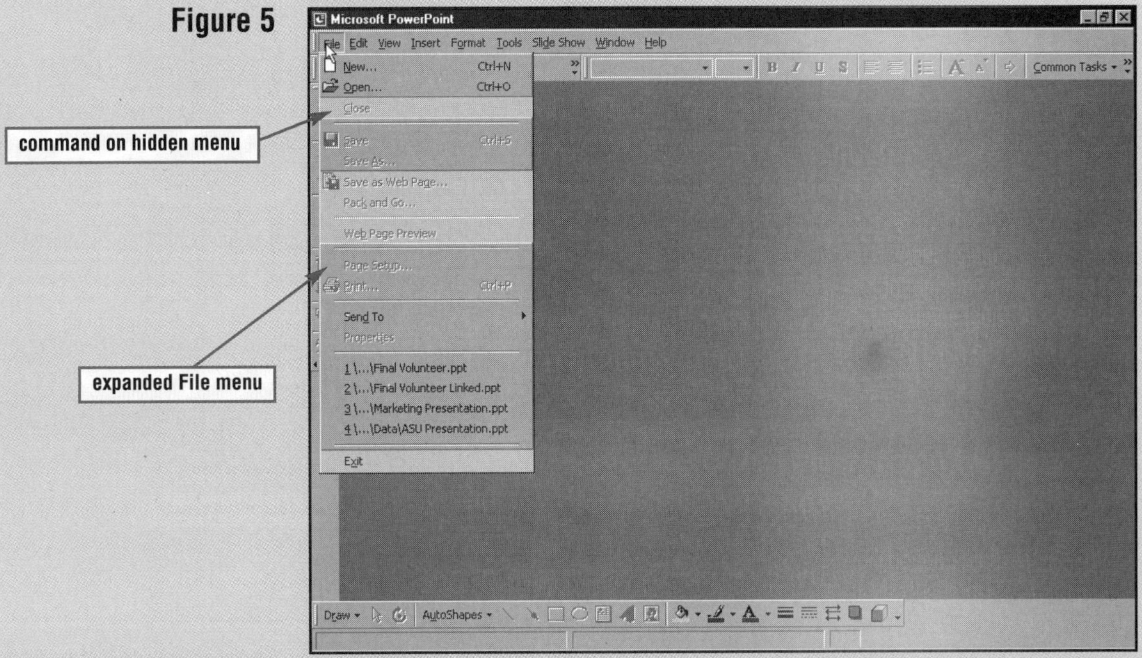

command on hidden menu

expanded File menu

The commands that are in the hidden menu appear on a light gray background. Once one menu is expanded, others are expanded automatically until you choose a command or perform another action.

2 ■ Point to each menu in the menu bar to see the expanded menu for each.

■ Point to the File menu again.

Many commands have images next to them so you can quickly associate the command with the image. The same image appears on the toolbar button for that feature.

Menus may include the following features, (not all menus include all features):

Feature	Meaning
Ellipses (...)	Indicates a dialog box will be displayed.
▶	Indicates a cascading menu will be displayed.
Dimmed	Indicates the command is not available for selection until certain other conditions are met.
Shortcut key	A key or key combination that can be used to execute a command without using the menu.
Checkmark ✔	Indicates a toggle type of command. Selecting it turns the feature on or off. A checkmark indicates the feature is on.

Once a menu is open, you can *select* a command from the menu by pointing to it. A colored highlight bar, called the **selection cursor**, appears over the selected command. If the selected command line displays a right-facing arrow, a submenu of commands automatically appears when the command is selected. This is commonly called a **cascading menu**.

3 ■ Point to the Send To command to display the cascading menu.

Your screen should be similar to Figure 6.

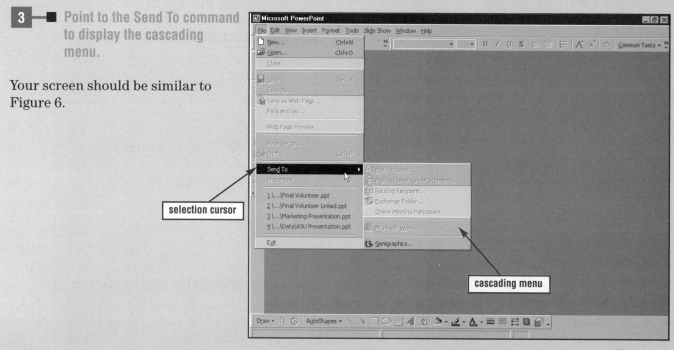

Figure 6

You can also type the underlined command letter to choose a command. If the command is already selected, you can press ←Enter to choose it.

Then to *choose* a command you click on it. When the command is chosen, the associated action is performed. You will use a command in the Help menu to access the Microsoft Office Assistant and Help feature.

4 ■ Point to Help.

■ Choose Show the Office Assistant.

If the Assistant does not appear, your school has disabled this feature. If this is the case, Choose Help/Microsoft PowerPoint Help and skip to the section Using Help.

If the Office Assistant feature is on this command does not appear on the Help menu and the Office Assistant should already be displayed on your screen.

Your screen should be similar to Figure 7.

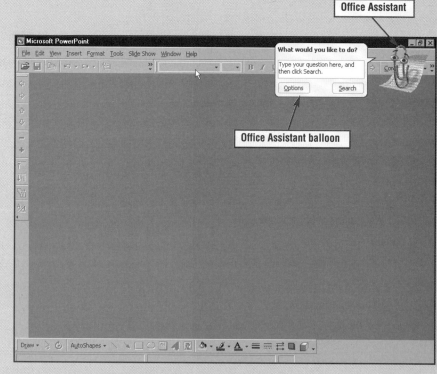

Figure 7

The command to display the assistant has been executed and the Office Assistant character is displayed. Because there are a variety of Assistant characters, your screen may display a different character than is shown here.

Using the Office Assistant

When the Office Assistant is on, it automatically suggests help topics as you work. It anticipates what you are going to do and then makes suggestions on how to perform a task. In addition, you can activate the Assistant at any time to get help on features in the Office application you are using. When active, the Office Assistant balloon appears and displays a prompt and a text box in which you can type the topic you want help on.

1 ▪— ▪ If necessary, click the Office Assistant character to activate it.

You will ask the Office Assistant to provide information on the different ways you can get help while using the program.

2 ▪— ▪ Type **How do I get help?**

▪ Click [Search] .

Your screen should be similar to Figure 8.

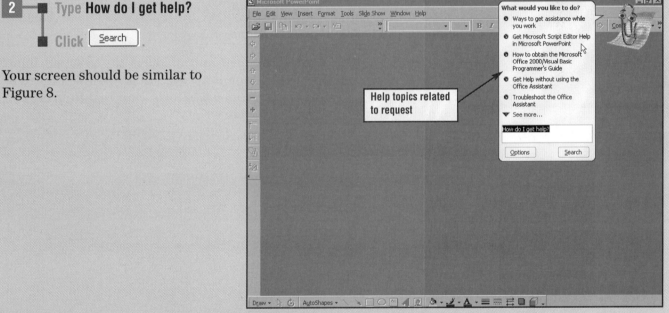

Figure 8

The balloon displays a list of related topics from which you can select.

3 ■ Click "Ways to get assistance while you work."

> If this topic is not displayed, select "See more…".

Your screen should be similar to Figure 9.

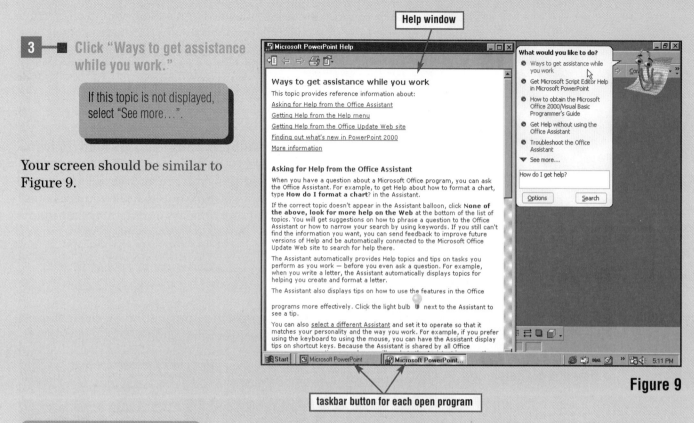

Figure 9

taskbar button for each open program

You can also press [F1] to open Help if the Office Assistant is not on.

The Help program has been opened and displays the selected topic. Because Help is a separate program it appears in its own window. The taskbar displays a button for both open windows. Now that Help is open, you no longer need to see the Assistant.

4 ■ Click [Search].

■ Select Use the Office Assistant to clear the checkmark.

■ Click [OK].

■ Click [Microsoft PowerPoint Help] in the taskbar to switch back to the Help window.

Additional Information

The [Options] button is used to change the Office Assistant settings to provide different levels of help, or to select a different Assistant character.

Using Help

In the Help window, the toolbar buttons help you use different Help features and navigate within Help. The ⟨≣ Show button displays the Help tabs frame.

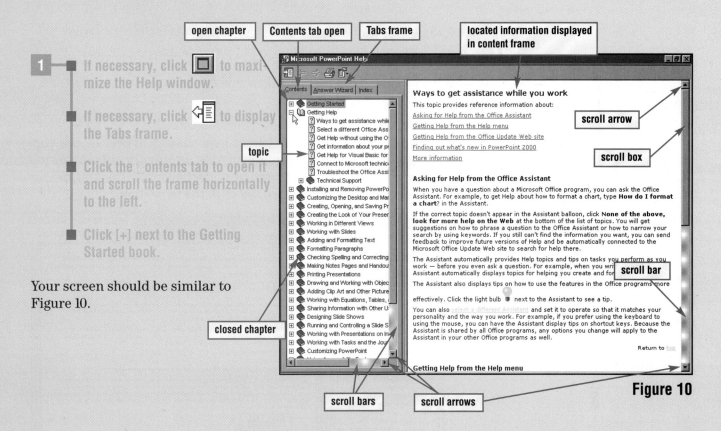

Figure 10

1 If necessary, click ▣ to maximize the Help window.

■ If necessary, click ◁▤ to display the Tabs frame.

■ Click the Contents tab to open it and scroll the frame horizontally to the left.

■ Click [+] next to the Getting Started book.

Your screen should be similar to Figure 10.

The Help window is divided into two vertical frames. **Frames** divide a window into separate, scrollable areas that can display different information. The left frame in the Help window is the **Tabs frame**. The three folder-like tabs, Contents, Index and Search, in the left frame are used to access the three different means of getting Help information. The open tab appears in front of the other tabs and displays the available options for the feature. The right frame, commonly called the **content frame**, displays the located information.

The Contents tab displays a table of contents listing of topics in Help. Clicking on an item preceded with a ◆ opens a "chapter" which expands to display additional "chapters" or specific Help topics. Chapters are preceded with a ▣ icon and topics with a ▣ icon.

The content frame displays the selected help topic. It contains more information than can be displayed at one time. A **scroll bar** is used with a mouse to bring additional lines of information into view in a window. It consists of **scroll arrows** and a **scroll box**. Clicking the arrows moves the information in the direction of the arrows, allowing new information to be displayed in the space. You can also move to a general location within the area by dragging the scroll box up or down the scroll bar. The location of the scroll box on the scroll bar indicates your relative position within the area of available information. Scroll bars can run vertically along the right side or horizontally along the bottom of a window. The vertical scroll bar is used to move vertically and the horizontal scroll bar moves horizontally in the space.

2 Scroll the content frame using the scroll bar to the bottom of the Help topic.

Scroll back to the top of the Help topic.

USING A HYPERLINK

Another way to move in Help is to click a hyperlink. A **hyperlink** is a connection to a location in the current document, another document, or the World Wide Web. It appears as colored or underlined text. Clicking the hyperlink moves to the location associated with the hyperlink.

The mouse pointer appears as 🖑 when pointing to a hyperlink.

1 Click the Asking for Help from the Office Assistant hyperlink.

Your screen should be similar to Figure 11.

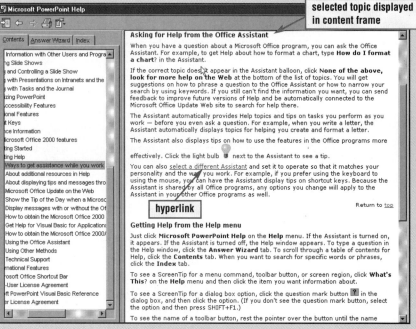

Figure 11

Help quickly jumps to the selected topic and displays the topic heading at the top of the frame.

2 Read the information displayed on this topic.

Click the select a different Assistant hyperlink.

Your screen should be similar to Figure 12.

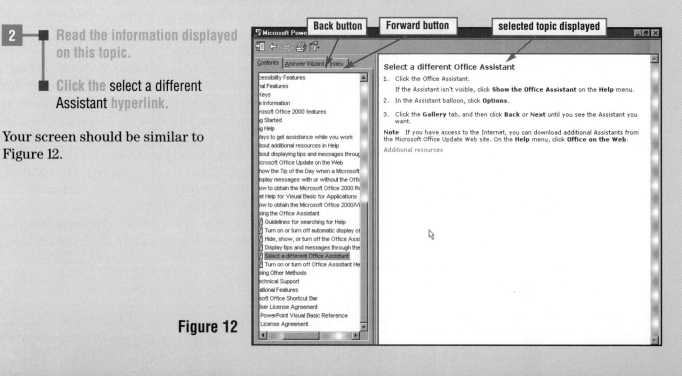

Figure 12

The help topic about selecting a different Assistant is displayed. Notice the Contents list now highlights this topic indicating it is the currently selected topic. Other hyperlinks will display a definition of a term in a popup box.

To quickly return to the previous topic,

The ⇨ Forward button is available after using ⇦ Back and can be used to move to the next viewed topic.

3 ── ■ Click ⇦ Back.

The previous topic is displayed again.

USING THE INDEX TAB

To search for Help information by entering a word or phrase for a topic, you can use the Index tab.

1 ── ■ Open the Index tab.

Your screen should be similar to Figure 13.

Index tab

enter word or phrase to locate

alphabetical list of Help keywords

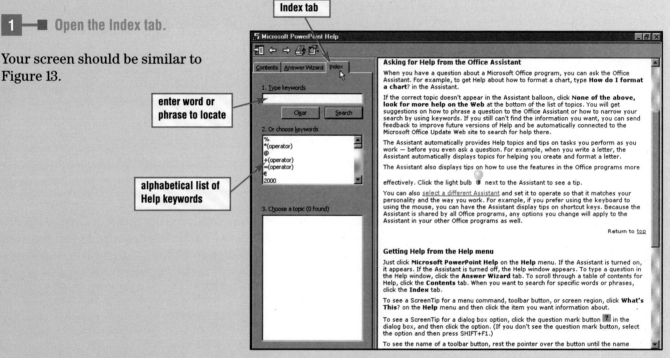

Figure 13

The Index tab consists of a text box where you can type a word or phrase that best describes the topic you want to locate and a list box displaying a complete list of Help keywords in alphabetical order. You want to find information about using the Index tab.

2 ── ■ Type **index** in the text box.

keyword list (2) displays word that matches as close as possible word entered (1)

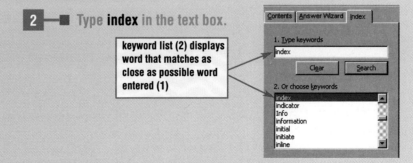

The keyword list jumps to the word index. To locate all Help topics containing this word,

3 ── ■ Click [Search] .

Your screen should be similar to Figure 14.

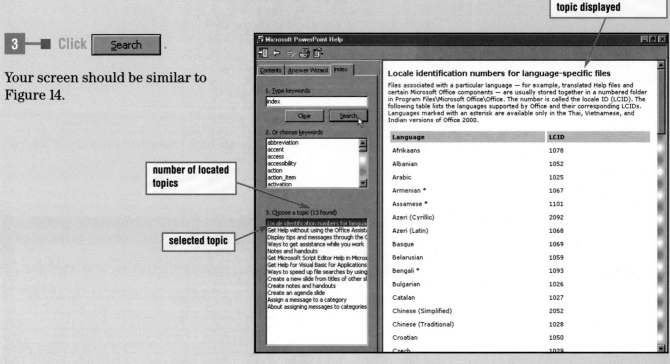

information for selected topic displayed

number of located topics

selected topic

Figure 14

The topic list has located 13 Help topics containing this word and displays the information on the first topic in the content frame. However, many of the located topics are not about the Help Index feature. To narrow the search more, you can add another word to the keyword text box.

4 ■ Following the word index in the keyword text box type **help**.

■ Click [Search] .

Your screen should be similar to Figure 15.

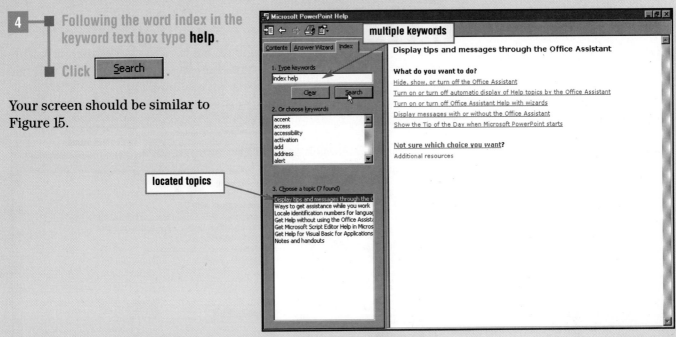

Figure 15

Now only 7 topics were located that contain both keywords.

5 ■ Click the "Get Help without using the Office Assistant" topic.

■ Read the information on this topic.

Your screen should be similar to Figure 16.

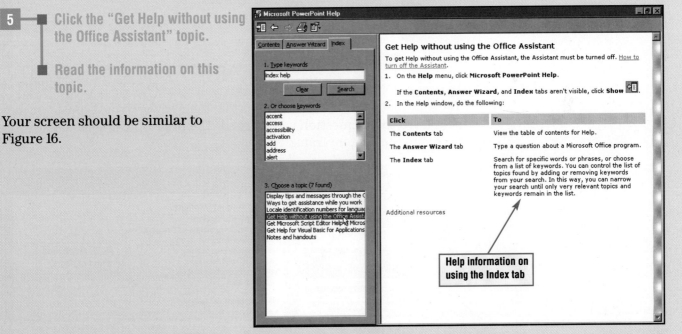

Figure 16

Using the AnswerWizard

Another way to locate Help topics is to use the AnswerWizard tab. This feature works just like the OfficeAssistant to locate topics. You will use this method to locate Help information on toolbars.

1 ■ Open the **A**nswer Wizard tab.

■ Type **How do toolbars work?** in the text box.

■ Click   Search   .

Additional Information

The search term does not need to be worded as a question. It can also be a word or phrase.

Your screen should be similar to Figure 17.

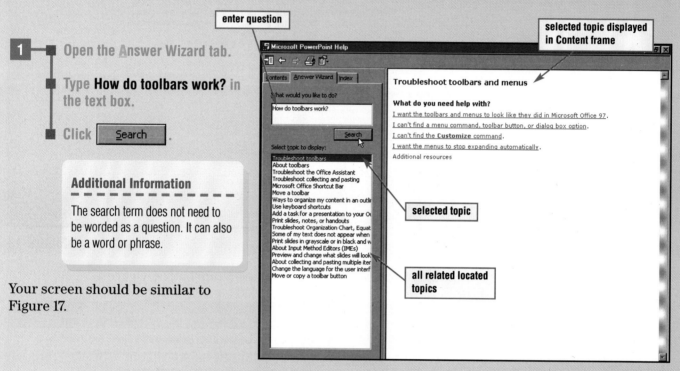

Figure 17

The topic list box displays all topics that the AnswerWizard considers may be related to the question you entered. The first topic is selected and displayed in the content frame.

2 ■ Click "About toolbars" from the topic list.

Your screen should be similar to Figure 18.

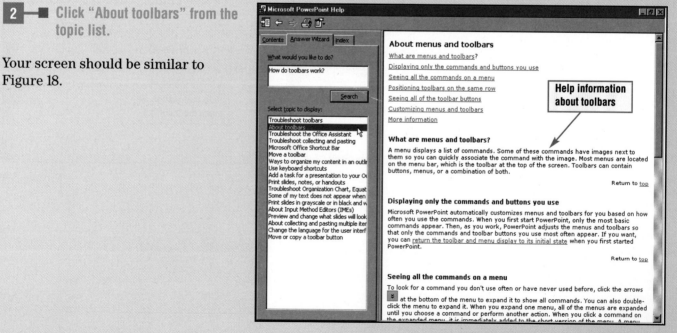

Figure 18

3 ■ Click 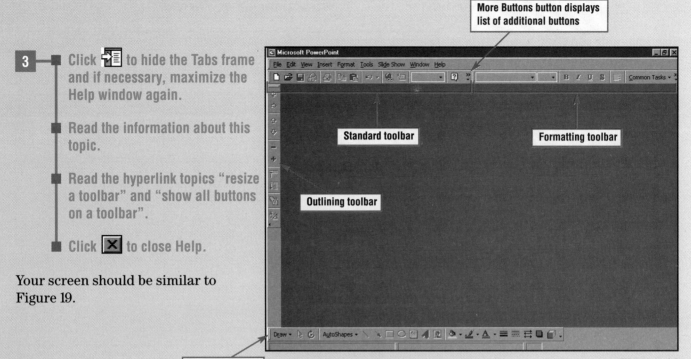 to hide the Tabs frame and if necessary, maximize the Help window again.

■ Read the information about this topic.

■ Read the hyperlink topics "resize a toolbar" and "show all buttons on a toolbar".

■ Click ☒ to close Help.

Your screen should be similar to Figure 19.

Figure 19

The Help window is closed and the PowerPoint window is displayed again.

Using Toolbars

While using Office 2000, you will see that many toolbars open automatically as different tasks are performed. Toolbars initially display the basic buttons. Like menus they are personalized automatically … displaying those buttons you use frequently and hiding others. The More Buttons ⟩ button located at the end of a toolbar displays a drop-down button list of those buttons that are not displayed. When you use a button from this list, it then is moved to the toolbar and a button that has not been used recently is moved to the More Buttons list.

Initially PowerPoint displays two toolbars, Standard and Formatting, on one row below the menu bar. (See Figure 19.) The Standard toolbar contains buttons that are used to complete the most frequently used menu commands. The Formatting toolbar contains buttons that are used to change the appearance or format of the presentation. Additionally, your screen may display two other toolbars. Outlining along the left edge of the workspace and Drawing along the bottom of the workspace. If you right-click on a toolbar the toolbar shortcut menu is displayed. Using this menu you can specify which toolbars are displayed. To see which toolbars are open,

Additional Information

Most of the toolbar buttons are dimmed because they are not available for use until a presentation is open.

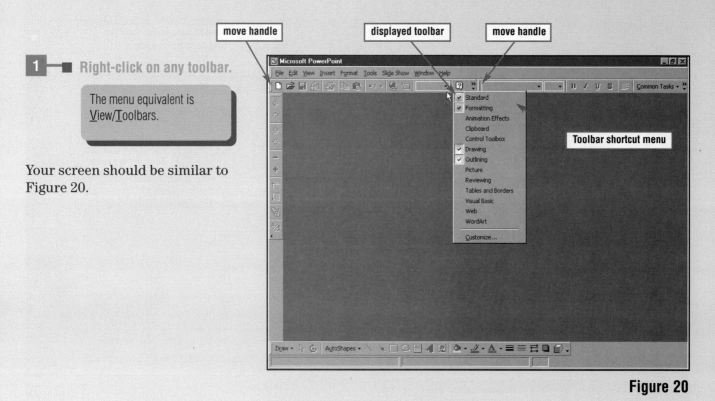

1 ■ Right-click on any toolbar.

The menu equivalent is View/Toolbars.

Your screen should be similar to Figure 20.

Figure 20

The Toolbar shortcut menu displays a list of toolbar names. Those that are currently displayed are checked. Clicking on a toolbar name from the list will display it onscreen. Likewise, clicking on a checked toolbar will hide the toolbar.

2 ■ If necessary, make the appropriate selections to display only the Standard, Formatting, Drawing, and Outlining toolbars.

There should now be four open toolbars. When a toolbar is opened, it may appear docked or floating. When **docked** they are fixed to an edge of the window and displays the move handle . Dragging this bar up or down allows you to move the toolbar. If multiple toolbars share the same row, dragging the bar left or right adjusts the size of the toolbar. If docked, a toolbar can occupy a row by itself or several can be on a row together. When floating they appear in a separate window that can be moved by dragging the title bar.

3 ■ Drag the move handle of the Standard toolbar into the workspace.

The mouse pointer appears as ✛ when you point to the ⬚ of any toolbar.

Your screen should be similar to Figure 21.

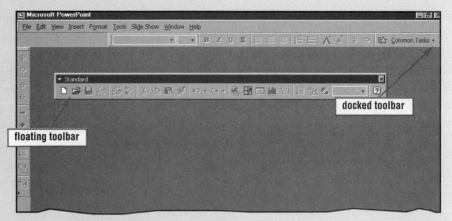

floating toolbar

docked toolbar

Figure 21

The Standard toolbar is now floating and can be moved to any location in the window by dragging the toolbar title bar. If you move it to the edge of the window, it will attach to that location and become a docked toolbar. A floating toolbar can also be sized by dragging the edge of the toolbar.

4 ■ Move the floating toolbar to the left end of the row below the menu bar.

■ If necessary move the Formatting toolbar to the right end of the same row as the Standard toolbar.

Your screen should be similar to Figure 22.

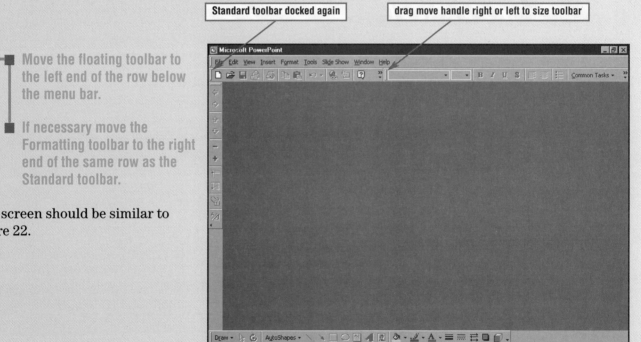

Standard toolbar docked again

drag move handle right or left to size toolbar

Figure 22

The two toolbars now occupy a single row. The size of each toolbar can be adjusted to show more or fewer buttons by dragging the move handle.

Additional Information

Double-clicking the bar when multiple toolbars share the same row minimizes or maximizes the toolbar size.

5 ■ Drag the ⬚ of the Formatting toolbar to the right or left as needed until each bar occupies approximately half the row space.

To quickly identify the toolbar buttons, you can display the button name by pointing to the button.

6 Point to any button on the Standard toolbar to see the ScreenTip displaying the button name.

Exiting an Office Application

The Exit command on the File menu can be used to quit most Windows programs. In addition, you can click the ☒ Close button in the application window title bar.

1 Click ☒ Close.

The application window is closed and the desktop is visible again.

Command Summary

Command	Shortcut Keys	Button	Action
Start/Programs			Opens program menu
File/Exit	Alt + F4	☒	Exits PowerPoint program
View/Toolbars			Hides or displays toolbars
Help/Microsoft PowerPoint Help	F1		Opens Help window
Help/Show the Office Assistant.			Displays Office Assistant.

Key Terms

Overview

What Is a Presentation Program?

You are in a panic! Tomorrow you are to make a presentation and you want it to be good. To the rescue comes a powerful tool: graphics presentation programs. These programs are designed to help you create an effective presentation, whether to the board of directors of your company or to your fellow classmates. An effective presentation gets your point across clearly and in an interesting manner.

Definition of Graphics Presentation Programs

Graphics presentation programs are designed to help you produce a high-quality presentation that is both interesting to the audience and effective in its ability to convey your message. A presentation can be as simple as overhead transparencies or as sophisticated as an onscreen electronic display. Graphics presentation programs can produce black-and-white or

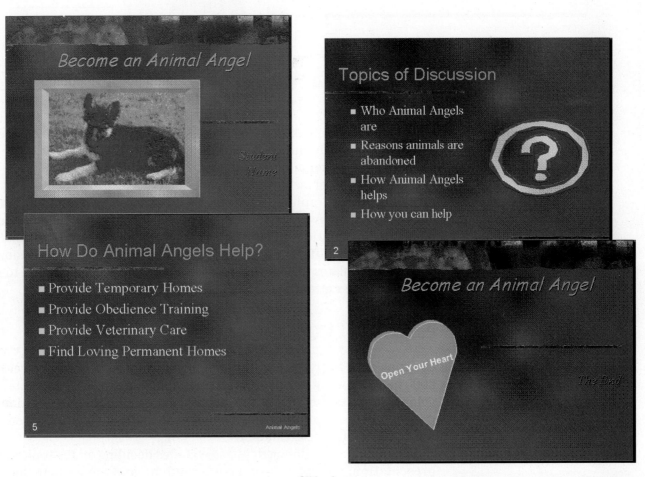

Slide show

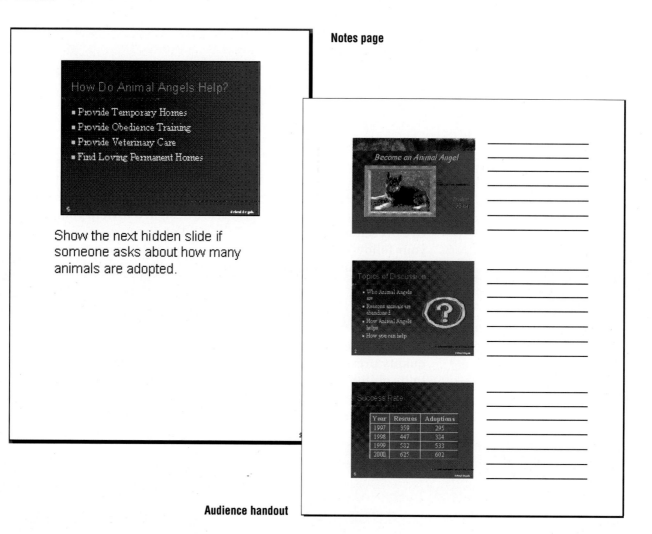

Notes page

Show the next hidden slide if someone asks about how many animals are adopted.

Audience handout

color overhead transparencies, 35mm slides, onscreen electronic presentations, called slide shows, Web pages for Web use, and support materials for both the speaker and the audience.

The graphics presentation program includes features such as text handling, outlining, graphing, drawing, animations, clip art, and multimedia support. With a few keystrokes you can quickly change, correct, and update the presentation. In addition, graphics presentation programs suggest layouts for different types of presentations and offer professionally designed templates to help you produce a presentation that is sure to keep your audience's attention.

PowerPoint 2000 Features

Creating an effective presentation is a complicated process. PowerPoint 2000 helps simplify this process by providing assistance in the content development phase, as well as the layout and design phase. In addition, the program helps to produce the support materials you can use when making a presentation to an audience.

The content development phase includes deciding on the topic of your presentation, the organization of the content, and the ultimate message you want to convey to the audience. As an aid in this phase, PowerPoint

Additional Information

PowerPoint 2000 includes an on-line tutorial that provides an introduction to PowerPoint. It is available on the program CD-ROM. Your school may have also made the tutorial available on the network.

2000 helps you organize your thoughts based on the type of presentation you are making. Several common types of presentations sell a product or idea, suggest a strategy, or report on the progress of a program. Based on the type of presentation, the program suggests ideas and organization tips. For example, if you are making a presentation on the progress of a sales campaign, the program would suggest that you enter text on the background of the sales campaign on the first "page," or slide; the current status of the campaign as the next slide; and accomplishments, schedule, issues and problems, and where you are heading on subsequent slides.

The layout of each slide is the next important decision. Again the program helps you by suggesting text layout features such as title placement, bullets, and columns. You can also incorporate graphs of data, tables, organizational charts, clip art, and other special text effects in the slides.

Also PowerPoint 2000 includes professionally designed templates to further enhance the appearance of your slides. These templates include features that standardize the appearance of all the slides in your presentation. Professionally selected combinations of text and background colors, common typefaces (fonts) and sizes, borders, and other art designs take the worry out of much of the design layout.

Once you have written and designed the slides, you can then have the slides made into black-and-white or color overhead transparencies or 35mm slides. Alternatively, you can use the slides in an onscreen electronic presentation or a Web page for use on the Web. An electronic presentation uses the computer to display the slides on an overhead projection screen. When using this type of presentation, many programs also include a rehearsal feature. This feature lets you practice and time your presentation. The length of time to display each slide can be set and your entire presentation can be completed within the allotted time. A presentation can be modified to display on a Web site and run using a Web browser.

Finally, PowerPoint 2000 also allows you to produce printouts of the materials you have created. You can print an outline of the text showing the titles of the slides and main text but not the art. The outline allows you to check the organizational logic of your presentation. You can also print speaker notes that you can refer to while making your presentation. These notes generally consist of a small printout of each slide with any notes on topics you want to discuss while the slides are displayed. Finally, you can create printed handouts of the slides for the audience. The audience can refer to the slide and make notes on the page as you speak.

Case Study for PowerPoint Tutorials

You have volunteered to help out at a local charity organization, Animal Angels. Animal Angels rescues unwanted pets from local animal shelters and finds foster homes for them until a suitable adoptive family can be found. Because of your computer skills, you have been selected to create a powerful and persuasive presentation to entice the community to volunteer.

The organization has recently purchased Microsoft PowerPoint 2000. You will use this package to create the presentation.

Before You Begin

To the Student

The following assumptions have been made:

■   The Microsoft PowerPoint 2000 program has been properly installed on the hard disk of your computer system. A mouse is also installed.

■   Your student data disk contains the files needed to complete the series of tutorials. These files are supplied by your instructor.

■   You are already familiar with how to use Windows and a mouse.

To the Instructor

By default, Office 2000 installs the most commonly used components and leaves others, to be installed when first accessed. It is assumed that these additional features have been installed prior to students using the tutorials.

Please be aware that the following settings are assumed to be in effect for the PowwerPoint 2000 program. These assumptions are necessary so that the screens and directions in the manual are accurate.

■   The Office Assistant feature is not on. (Click on the Assistant, click Options... , and clear the Use the Office Assistant option.)

■   The Normal view is on. Zoom is 100 percent. (Use View/Normal.)

■   The Standard, Formatting, Outlining, and Drawing toolbars are on.

■   The Clip gallery is fully installed. If the clip art frame.wmf used in Tutorial 1 is not available in the Clip Gallery, use Insert/Picture/Clip Art/Import Clips and add it to the Borders and Frames category with a keyword of "frame."

■   The Automatic Spelling check feature is on. (Use Tools/Option/Check style.)

■   The default Style options are in effect. (Use Tools/Option/Check style.)

■   The feature to check style is on. (Use Tools/Options/Check style/Style Options/Defaults.)

■   The default Style options are in effect. (Use Tools/Options/Check spelling as you type.)

■   All the options in the View tab are selected. (Use Tools/Options/View.)

In addition, all figures in the manual reflect the use of a standard VGA display monitor set at 800 by 600. If another monitor setting is used, there may be more or fewer lines of text displayed in the windows than in the figures. This setting can be changed using Windows setup.

Microsoft Office 2000 Shortcut Bar

The Microsoft Office 2000 Shortcut Bar (shown below) may be displayed automatically on the Windows desktop. Commonly, it appears on the right side of the desktop, or it may appear in other locations depending upon your setup. This is because the Shortcut Bar can be customized to display other toolbar buttons.

The Office Shortcut Bar makes it easy to open existing documents or to create new documents using one of the Microsoft Office applications. It can also be used to send e-mail, add a task to a to-do list, schedule appointments using Schedule[+], or add contacts or notes.

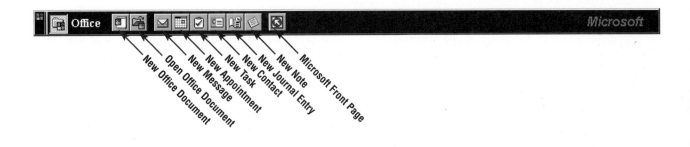

Instructional Conventions

Hands-on instructions you are to perform appear as a sequence of numbered blue steps. Within each step, a series of pink bullets identifies the specific actions that must be performed. Step numbering begins new within each main topic heading throughout the tutorial.

Command sequences you are to issue appear following the word "Choose." Each menu command selection is separated by a /. If the menu command can be selected by typing a letter of the command, the letter will appear underlined. Items that need to be selected will follow the word "Select" and appear in black text. You can select items with the mouse or directional keys.

EXAMPLE

1 ■ Choose File/Open.

   ■ Select Volunteer1.ppt.

Commands that can be initiated using a button and the mouse appear following the word "Click." The icon (and the icon name if the icon does not include text) is displayed following "Click." The menu equivalent and keyboard shortcut appear in a margin note when the action is first introduced.

The menu equivalent is **F**ile/**O**pen and the keyboard shortcut is `Ctrl` + O.

EXAMPLE

1 ─■ Click  Open.

Black text identifies items you need to select or move to. Information you are asked to type appears in black and bold.

EXAMPLE

1 ─■ Move to the A in Announcing.

■ Type **How Do I Become an Animal Angel?**.

Creating a Presentation

Case Study You have volunteered to help out at a local charity organization, Animal Angels. Animal Angels rescues unwanted pets from local animal shelters and finds foster homes for them until a suitable adoptive family can be found. Because of your computer skills, you have been selected to create a powerful and persuasive presentation to entice the community to volunteer.

Competencies

After completing this tutorial, you will know how to:

1. Use the AutoContent Wizard to create a presentation.
2. View and edit a presentation.
3. Save and open a presentation.
4. Use the spelling checker.
5. Delete, move, and insert slides.
6. Set and use tabs.
7. Run a slide show.
8. Change fonts and font size.
9. Size and move objects.
10. Insert pictures and clip art.
11. Preview and print a presentation.

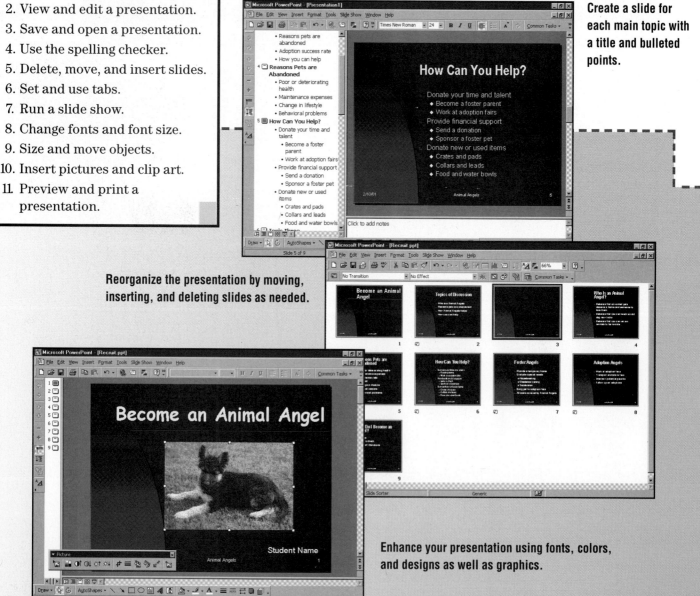

Create a slide for each main topic with a title and bulleted points.

Reorganize the presentation by moving, inserting, and deleting slides as needed.

Enhance your presentation using fonts, colors, and designs as well as graphics.

The agency director has just informed you that you need to preview the presentation at the weekly staff meeting tomorrow, and has asked you to present a draft of the presentation by noon today.

Although we would all like to think that our message is the core of the presentation, the presentation materials we use can determine whether or not the message reaches the audience. To help you create the presentation, you will use PowerPoint 2000, a graphics presentation application that is designed to create presentation materials such as slides, overheads, and handouts. Using PowerPoint you can create a high-quality and interesting onscreen presentation with pizzazz that will dazzle your audience.

Become an Animal Angel

2/10/01

How Do I Become an Angel?

Call us
Send a check
Drop off Donations

2/10/01

Adoption Angels

Work at adoption fairs
Transport animals to fairs
Interview potential parents

Topics of Discussion

Who are Animal Angels
Reasons pets are abandoned
How Animal Angels helps

2

Foster Angels

Provide a temporary home
Evaluate special needs
◆ Housebreaking

8

Animal Angels History

Year Event
1990 Founded by Ed Wilton
1991 Built first shelter
1996 Began volunteer program
1999 Expanded to 10 shelters

How Can You Help?

Donate your time and talent
◆ Foster parents
◆ Work at adoption fairs
ipport
pet
d items

ngels

7

Reasons Pets are Abandoned

2/10/01

Poor or deteriorating health
Maintenance expenses
◆ Veterinary bills
◆ Food
Change in lifestyle
Medical reasons
Behavioral problems

2/10/01   Animal Angels   5

Who Is an Animal Angel?

Believes that unwanted pets deserve a home and someone to love them
Believes that you can teach an old dog new tricks
Believes that you can retrain animals to be lovable

owls

6

2/10/01   Animal Angels   4

Concept Overview

The following concepts will be introduced in this tutorial:

1 **Presentation Development** The development of a presentation follows several steps: plan, create, edit, enhance, and rehearse.

2 **Types of Presentation Styles** A PowerPoint presentation can be made using five different styles: onscreen presentations, Web presentations, black-and-white or color overheads, and 35mm slides.

3 **Slide** A slide is an individual "page" of your presentation. The first slide of a presentation is the title slide. Additional slides are used to support each main point in your presentation.

4 **AutoCorrect** The AutoCorrect feature makes some basic assumptions about the text you are typing and, based on these assumptions, automatically identifies and/or corrects the entry.

5 **Automatic Spelling Check** The automatic spelling checker feature advises you of misspelled words as you create and edit a presentation, and proposes possible corrections.

6 **Fonts** A font is a set of characters with a specific design. Using fonts as a design element can add interest to your presentation.

7 **Graphics** A graphic is an object such as a drawing or picture that can be added to a slide.

Exploring the PowerPoint Window

The Animal Angels organization has just purchased the graphics presentation program, Microsoft PowerPoint 2000. Using this program you should have no problem creating a presentation for tomorrow's staff meeting.

1 If necessary, turn on your computer and put your data disk in drive A (or the appropriate drive for your system).

See Introducing Common Office 2000 Features for information on how to start the application and for a discussion of features that are common to all Office 2000 applications.

■ Start the Microsoft PowerPoint 2000 application.

If a ▢ Shortcut to Powerpnt.exe button is displayed on your desktop, you can double-click on the button to start the program.

Your screen should be similar to Figure 1-1.

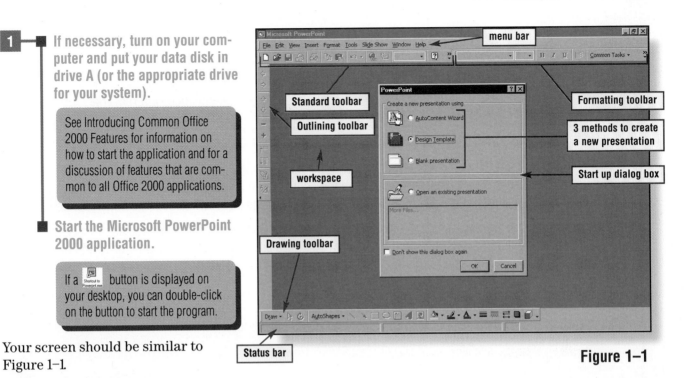

Figure 1-1

Because the Office 2000 applications remember settings that were on when the program was last exited, your screen may look slightly different.

Additional Information

There are 13 different PowerPoint toolbars.

The PowerPoint application window with the startup dialog box open in it is displayed. The menu bar below the title bar displays the PowerPoint program menu. It consists of nine menus that provide access to the commands and features you will use to create and modify a presentation document.

Normally located below the menu bar are the Standard and Formatting toolbars. The **Standard toolbar** contains buttons that are used to complete the most frequently used menu commands. The **Formatting toolbar** contains buttons that are used to change the appearance or format of the document. In addition, two toolbars, Outlining and Drawing, may be displayed if they were on when the program was last exited. The **Outlining toolbar** is commonly displayed along the left edge of the window. It contains buttons that are used to rearrange the content of your presentation. The **Drawing toolbar** is displayed along the bottom edge of the window. It contains buttons that are used to enhance text and create shapes.

The large area containing the startup dialog box is the **workspace**. It is where your presentations are displayed as you create and edit them. The status bar at the bottom of the PowerPoint window displays messages and information about various PowerPoint settings. Currently the status bar is empty. In addition, your screen may display the Office Assistant.

Refer to the Introducing Common Office 2000 features section to learn how to turn off the Assistant.

2 If necessary turn off the Office Assistant.

Planning a Presentation

During your presentation you will present information about the Animal Angels organization and why someone should want to volunteer. As you prepare to create a new presentation, you should follow several basic steps.

Concept ① Presentation Development

The development of a presentation follows several steps: plan, create, edit, enhance, and rehearse.

Plan: The first step in planning a presentation is to understand its purpose. You also need to find out the length of time you have to speak, who the audience is, what type of room you will be in, and what kind of audiovisual equipment is available. These factors have an impact on the type of presentation you will create.

Create: To begin creating your presentation, develop the content by typing your thoughts or notes into an outline. Each main idea in your presentation should have a supporting slide with a title and bulleted points.

Edit: While typing, you are bound to make typing and spelling errors that need to be corrected. This is one type of editing. Another is to revise the content of what you have entered to make it clearer, or to add or delete information. To do this, you might insert a slide, add or delete bulleted items, or move text to another location.

Enhance: You want to develop a presentation that grabs and holds the audience's attention. Choose a design that gives your presentation some dazzle. Wherever possible add graphics to replace or enhance text. Add effects that control how a slide appears and disappears, and that reveal text in a bulleted list one bullet at a time.

Rehearse: Finally, you should rehearse the delivery of your presentation. For a professional presentation, your delivery should be as polished as your materials. Use the same equipment that you will use when you give the presentation. Practice advancing from slide to slide and then back in case someone asks a question. If you have a mouse available, practice pointing or drawing on the slide to call attention to key points.

After rehearsing your presentation, you may find that you want to go back to the editing phase. You may change text, move bullets, or insert a new slide. Periodically, as you make changes, rehearse the presentation again to see how the changes affect your presentation. By the day of the presentation, you will be confident about your message and at ease with the materials.

The purpose of your presentation is to educate members of the community about the organization and to persuade many to volunteer. In addition, you want to impress the agency director by creating a professional presentation.

Creating the Presentation Using the AutoContent Wizard

The startup dialog box is used to specify how you want to start using the PowerPoint program. It includes three options that provide access to different methods for creating a new presentation. The **AutoContent Wizard** is a guided approach that helps you determine the content and organization of your presentation through a series of questions. Then it creates a presentation that contains suggested content and design based on the answers you provide. You can also create a new presentation beginning with a **design template**, which is a file containing predefined settings that de-

You will learn more about design templates in Tutorial 2.

termine the presentation's color scheme, fonts, and other design features. Finally, you can create a new presentation from scratch using the Blank Presentation option which sets color scheme, fonts, and other design features to default values. Since this is your first presentation created in PowerPoint, you will use the AutoContent Wizard.

Additional Information

If the Microsoft Office Suite is on your system and the Office Shortcut Bar is displayed, you can click 📝 Start a New Document and select the method you want to use to create a new presentation while loading the PowerPoint program.

1 ■ Select <u>A</u>utoContent Wizard.

■ Click | OK |.

The menu equivalent is <u>F</u>ile/<u>N</u>ew/ General/ AutoContent Wizard.

Your screen should be similar to Figure 1–2.

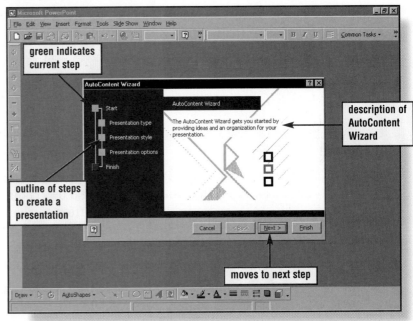

Figure 1–2

The opening dialog box of the AutoContent Wizard briefly describes how the feature works. As the AutoContent Wizard guides you through creating the presentation, it shows you which step you are on in the outline on the left side of the window. The green box identifies the current step. To move on to the next step,

2 ━■ Click   Next >   .

> You can also click the outline box on the left side to move directly to any step.

Your screen should be similar to Figure 1–3.

Figure 1–3

In the Presentation Type step, you are asked to select the type of presentation you are creating. PowerPoint includes 24 different types of presentations, each with a different recommended content and design. Each type is indexed under a category. Currently, only the presentation types in the General category are listed, and a descriptive name for each presentation type in this category appears in the list box.

3 ━■ Click on each category button to see the different presentation types in each category.

You will use the Generic presentation option.

4 ━■ Select Generic from the General category.

> The Generic option is also available under the All category.

■ Click   Next >   .

Your screen should be similar to Figure 1–4.

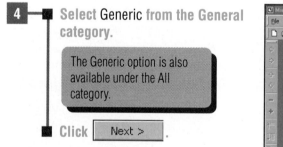

Figure 1–4

In the Presentation Style step, you select the type of output your presentation will use.

Concept ② Presentation Styles

A PowerPoint presentation can be made using five different styles: onscreen presentations, Web presentations, black-and-white or color overheads, and 35mm slides. The type of equipment that is available to you will have an impact on the type of presentation you create.

If you have computer projection equipment, which displays the current monitor image on a screen, you should create a full-color onscreen presentation. You can also design your onscreen presentation specifically for the World Wide Web, where a browser serves as the presentation tool. Often you will have access only to an overhead projector, in which case you can create color or black-and-white transparencies. Most laser printers will print your overheads directly on plastic transparencies, or you can print your slides and have transparencies made at a copy center. If you have access to a slide projector, you may want to use 35mm slides. You can send your presentation to a service bureau that will create the slides for you.

The room you will be using to make your presentation is equipped with computer projection equipment, so you will create an onscreen presentation. The Wizard selects the color scheme best suited to the type of output you select. Since On-screen presentation is the default selection, to accept it and move to the next step,

5 ■ Click  .

Your screen should be similar to Figure 1–5.

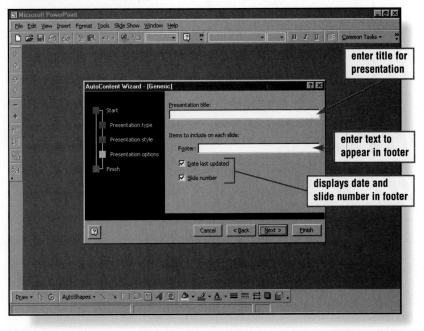

Figure 1–5

In the Presentation Options step, you are asked to enter some basic information that will appear on the title slide and in the footer of each slide in the presentation.

Concept ③ Slide

A **slide** is an individual "page" of your presentation. The first slide of a presentation is the title slide. It is used to introduce your presentation. Additional slides are used to support each main point in your presentation. The slides give the audience a visual summary of the words you speak, which helps them understand the content and keeps them entertained. The slides also help you, the speaker, organize your thoughts, and prompt you during the presentation.

You would like the name of the presentation to appear as the title on the first slide, and the name of the organization, date of the presentation, and the slide number to appear on the footer of each slide. A **footer** is text or graphics that appears at the bottom of each slide. Because the options to display the date that the presentation was last updated and slide number are already selected, you only need to enter the title text and footer text.

6 ■ Type **Become an Animal Angel** in the Presentation title text box.

> If you make a typing error, use the ⌜Backspace⌟ key to delete the characters to the left of the insertion point and then retype the correct text.

■ Type **Animal Angels** in the Footer text box.

■ Click   Next >   .

Your screen should be similar to Figure 1–6.

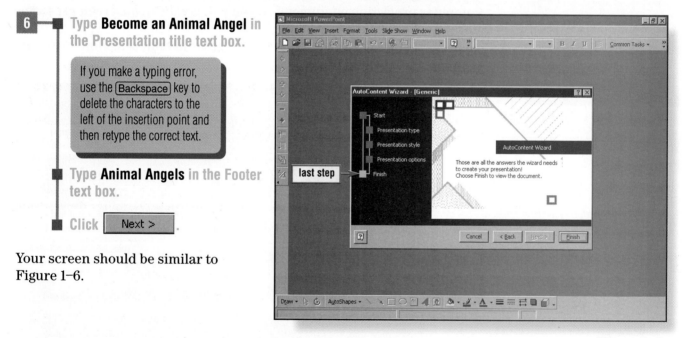

Figure 1–6

The step outline indicates you have entered all the information PowerPoint needs to create your presentation.

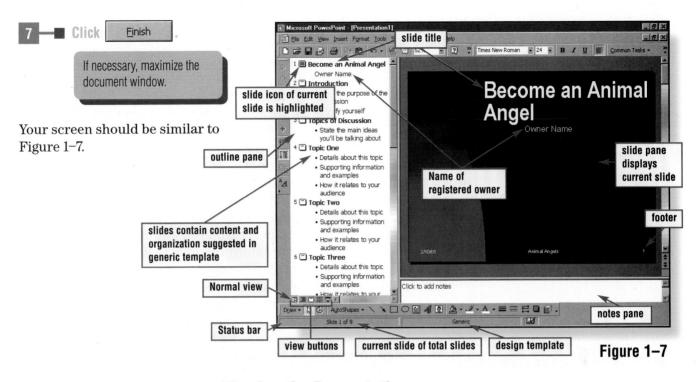

7 Click Finish .

If necessary, maximize the document window.

Your screen should be similar to Figure 1-7.

Figure 1-7

Viewing the Presentation

Based on your selections and entries, the AutoContent Wizard creates a presentation and displays it in a document window in the workspace. The presentation is initially displayed in Normal view. PowerPoint provides five different **views** you can use to look at and modify your presentation. Depending on what you are doing, one view may be preferable to another. The commands to change views are located on the View menu. In addition, the five view buttons to the left of the horizontal scroll bar can be used to quickly switch from one view to another. The menu commands, buttons, and views are described in the table below.

View	Command	Button	Description
Normal	**V**iew/**N**ormal		Provides three separate divisions of the window, called **panes** that allow you to work on all aspects of your presentation in one place. You enter content in the outline pane, enhance the presentation in the slide pane, and enter speaker notes in the notes pane.
Outline			Displays the outline and notes panes enlarged so you can concentrate on entering and editing the presentation's content. A miniature of the slide is also displayed.
Slide			The slide pane is enlarged so you can work on enhancing the slides.
Slide Sorter	**V**iew/Sli**d**e Sorter		Displays a miniature of each slide to make it easy to reorder slides, add special effects such as transitions, and sets timing between slides.
Slide Show	**V**iew/Slide Sho**w**		Displays each slide in final form using the full screen space so you can practice or present the presentation.

Additional Information

You can adjust the size the panes by dragging the pane borders.

Normal view is displayed by default because it is the main view you will use while creating a presentation. In Normal view, the outline pane, slide pane, and notes pane are displayed. This allows you to work on all components of your presentation in one convenient location. The outline pane displays in outline format the title and text for each slide in the presentation. This pane is used to organize and develop the content of your presentation.

To the left of each slide title in the outline pane is a slide icon ▭ and a number that identifies each slide. The icon of the current slide is highlighted, and the current slide is displayed in the slide pane. The text for the first slide consists of the title and the footer text you specified when using the AutoContent Wizard. Below the title, the name of the registered owner of the application program is displayed automatically. The other slides shown in the outline pane contain sample text that is included by the Wizard based upon the type of presentation you selected. The sample text suggests the content for each slide to help you organize your presentation's content. The status bar now displays the number of the current slide and total number of slides, and the name of the design template used.

The second main view that is used while creating a presentation is Slide Sorter view. To switch to this view,

1 ■ Click 🏢 Slide Sorter View.

> Pointing to a view button displays its name in a ScreenTip.

Your screen should be similar to Figure 1–8.

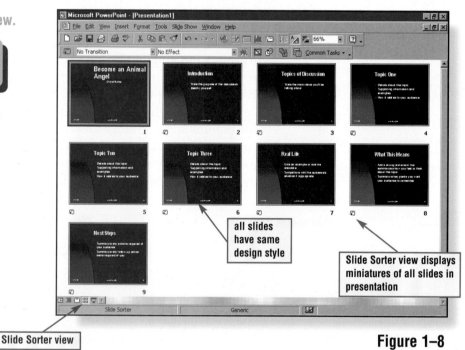

Figure 1–8

This view displays a miniature of each slide in the presentation in the window. You can now see that there are a total of nine slides in the presentation. All the slides use the same design style, associated with a generic presentation. The design style sets the background design and color, as well as the text style, color, and layout.

Additional Information

Normal view is often referred to as a tri-pane view because it displays three panes simultaneously.

2 ■ Click 🖾 to switch to Normal view again.

Editing a Presentation Using the Outline Pane

After creating a presentation using the AutoContent Wizard, you need to replace the sample text with the appropriate information for your presentation. It is easiest to make these changes in Normal view. First, you will make changes to the text in the outline pane. When working in the outline pane, it is helpful to have the Outlining toolbar displayed.

1 ■ If necessary, turn on the Outlining toolbar.

The first change you want to make is to select the owner name on the first slide and delete it. In the outline pane you can select text by dragging when the mouse pointer is an I-beam. In addition, you can quickly select an entire paragraph and all subparagraphs by triple-clicking on a line or by pointing to the left of the line and clicking when the mouse pointer is a . If you click the slide icon ⬚ to the right of the slide number, all text on the slide is selected. To remove the name,

2 ■ Click to the left of the owner name on slide 1 in the outline pane when the mouse pointer is a ✛.

■ Press Delete.

> If you accidentally drag selected text, it will move. To return it to its original location, use **E**dit/**U**ndo or click ↶▾ Undo immediately.

■ Click on slide 1 in the outline pane.

Your screen should be similar to Figure 1–9.

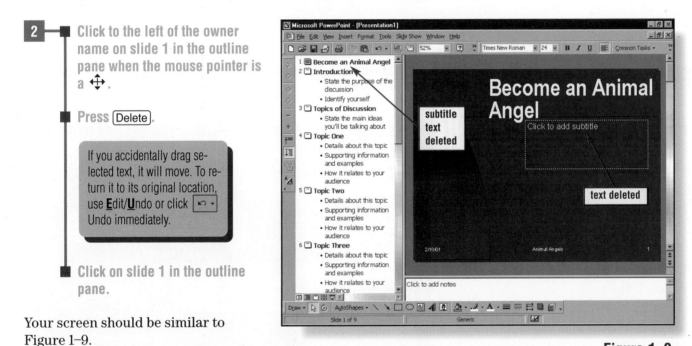

Figure 1–9

The text and entire line are removed. The slide in the slide pane also reflects the change made to the slide. The next change you want to make is in the Introduction slide. The sample text in this slide recommends that you enter an opening statement to explain the purpose of the discussion and to introduce yourself.

3 ── **Click on the slide 2 icon.**

Your screen should be similar to Figure 1–10.

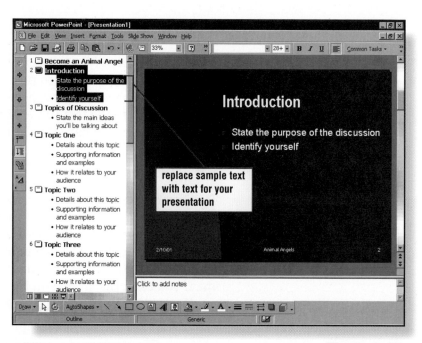

Figure 1–10

The slide pane now displays the second slide. You need to replace the sample text next to the first bullet with the text for your slide. To enter the purpose for your presentation,

4 ── **Select the sample text** State the purpose of the discussion.

■ **Type volunter (this word is intentionally misspelled).**

■ **Press** Spacebar.

Your screen should be similar to Figure 1–11.

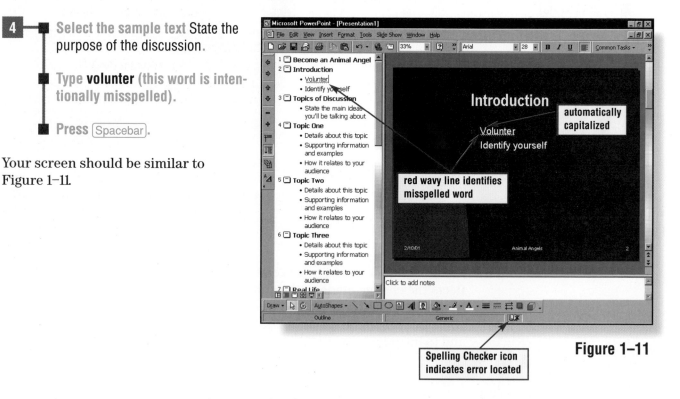

Spelling Checker icon indicates error located

Figure 1–11

As you make changes in the outline pane, the slide pane updates immediately. Also as you enter text, the program checks words for accuracy. First PowerPoint capitalized the first letter of the word. This is part of the AutoCorrect feature of Word.

Concept 4 AutoCorrect

The **AutoCorrect** feature makes some basic assumptions about the text you are typing and, based on these assumptions, automatically identifies and/or corrects the entry. The AutoCorrect feature automatically inserts proper capitalization at the beginning of sentences and the names of days of the week. It will also change to lowercase letters any words that were incorrectly capitalized due to the accidental use of the [Caps Lock] key. In addition, it also corrects many common spelling errors automatically.

The [ ] indicator means no spelling errors have been found.

Next PowerPoint identified the word as a misspelled word by underlining it with a wavy red line. In addition, the spelling indicator in the status bar appears as [ ], indicating the automatic spelling checker feature has found a spelling error.

Concept 5 Automatic Spelling Checker

The automatic spelling checker feature advises you of misspelled words as you create and edit a presentation, and proposes possible corrections. The spelling checker compares the word you type to a **main dictionary** of words supplied with the program. Although this dictionary includes most common words, it may not include proper names, technical terms, and so on. If the word does not appear in the main dictionary, the spelling checker checks the **custom dictionary**, a dictionary that you can create to hold words you commonly use but that are not included in the main dictionary. If the word does not appear in either dictionary, the program identifies it as misspelled by displaying a red wavy line below the word. You can then correct the misspelled word by editing it. Alternatively, you can display a list of suggested spelling corrections for that word and select the correct spelling from the list to replace the misspelled word in the presentation.

The spelling checker works just as in the other Microsoft Office 2000 applications.

Because you have discovered this error very soon after typing it, and you know that the correct spelling of this word is "volunteer," you can quickly correct it using [Backspace]. The [Backspace] key removes the character or space to the left of the insertion point; therefore, it is particularly useful when you are moving from right to left (backward) along a line of text. To correct this word, and continue entering the text for this slide,

As you type, an animated pen appears over the spelling indicator while the Spelling Checker is in the process of checking for errors.

5 ■ Press [Backspace] twice.

■ Type **er**

■ Press [Spacebar].

■ Type **Recrutment**

Again, the program has identified a word as misspelled. Another way to quickly correct a misspelled word is to select the correct spelling from a list of suggested spelling corrections displayed on the Spelling shortcut menu.

6 ━■ Right-click on the word in the
       outline pane to display the
       Spelling shortcut menu.

Your screen should be similar to
Figure 1–12.

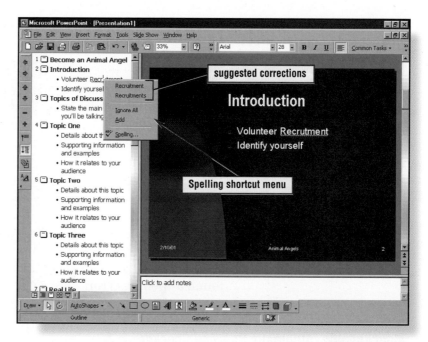

Figure 1–12

This menu displays two suggested correct spellings. The menu also includes several related menu options described below.

Option	Effect
Ignore All	Instructs PowerPoint to ignore the misspelling of this word throughout the rest of this session.
Add	Adds the word to the custom dictionary list. When a word is added to the custom dictionary, PowerPoint will always accept that spelling as correct.
Spelling	Starts the spelling checker to check the entire presentation. You will learn about this feature shortly.

Sometimes there are no suggested replacements because PowerPoint cannot locate any words in its dictionary that are similar in spelling; or the
suggestions are not correct. If this happens, you need to edit the word
manually. To replace the word with the correct spelling and to enter your
name on this slide,

7 ■ Choose Recruitment.

■ Select Identify yourself in the outline pane.

■ Type **your name**.

Your screen should be similar to Figure 1-13.

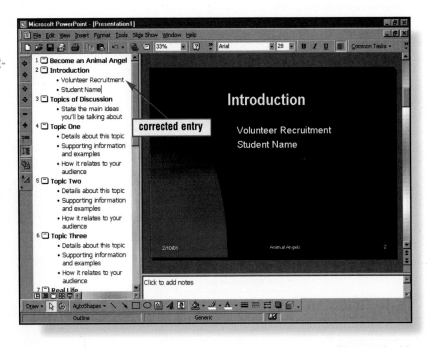

Figure 1-13

You are now ready to update the third slide in your presentation by entering the three main topics you will be discussing. You want to enter each topic on a separate bulleted line. The first bullet is already displayed and contains sample text that you will replace. To add additional lines and bullets, you simply press ←Enter.

8 ■ In slide 3 of the outline pane, select State the main ideas you'll be talking about.

■ Type **Reasons pets are abandoned**.

■ Press ←Enter.

■ Type **How you can help**.

■ Press ←Enter.

■ Type **Adoption success rate** (do not press ←Enter)

> If you need to remove an extra bullet and blank line, press Bksp twice.

Your screen should be similar to Figure 1-14.

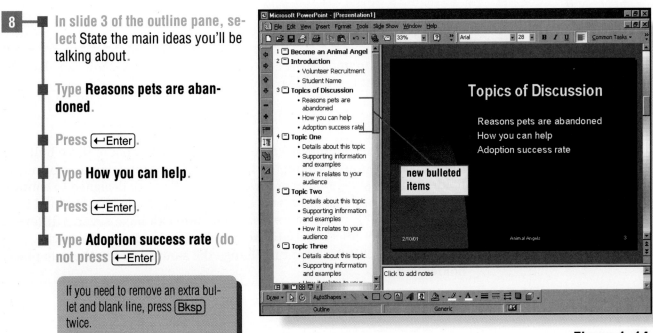

Figure 1-14

You realize that you entered the topics in the wrong order. You want to reverse the order of the second and third items in the list. A bulleted point can be moved easily by selecting it and dragging it to a new location, or by using the ⬆ Move Up or ⬇ Move Down buttons in the Outlining toolbar. To move the bulleted item on the current line up one line,

9 ━■ Click ⬆ Move Up.

Your screen should be similar to Figure 1–15.

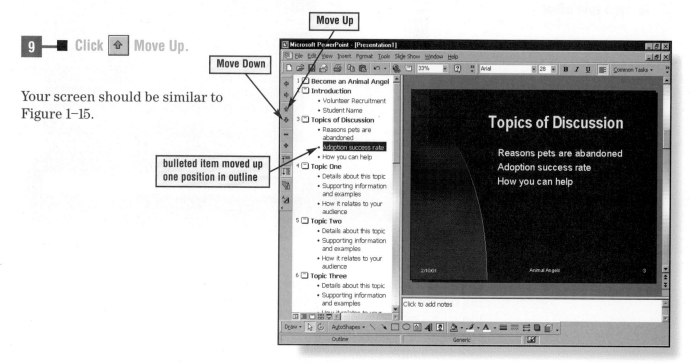

Figure 1–15

Editing in the Slide Pane

Next you want to update the content of the fourth slide. You can also edit the slide content in the slide pane.

1 ━■ Display slide 4 in the slide pane.

The fourth slide contains the title "Topic One" and a list of three bulleted items. The title and the bulleted list are two separate elements or placeholders on the slide. **Placeholders** are boxes that are designed to contain specific types of items or **objects** such as the slide title text, bulleted item text, charts, tables, and pictures. Each slide can have several different types of placeholders. To indicate which placeholder to work with, you must first select it. You want to change the sample text in the title placeholder first.

2 ▪ Click anywhere on the slide title text in the slide pane.

> To deselect a placeholder, click anywhere outside the selected placeholder.

Your screen should be similar to Figure 1–16.

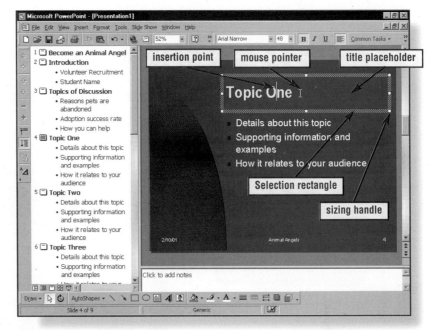

Figure 1–16

Additional Information

A dotted border around a selected object indicates you can format the box itself. Clicking the hatched border changes it to a dotted border.

The title placeholder is now a selected object and is surrounded with eight **sizing** or **solution handles** (boxes) and a **selection rectangle**. Dragging on the sizing handles changes the size of the placeholder. When the selection rectangle border appears hatched, this indicates you can enter, delete, select and format the text inside the box. An insertion point is displayed to show your location in the text and to allow you to select and edit the text. The mouse pointer appears as an I-beam to be used to position the insertion point. To enter the new title for this slide,

3 ▪ Select the title text.

> Drag to select a portion of the text, double-click to select a word, or triple-click to select a line.

▪ Type **Reasons Pets are Abandoned**.

Your screen should be similar to Figure 1–17.

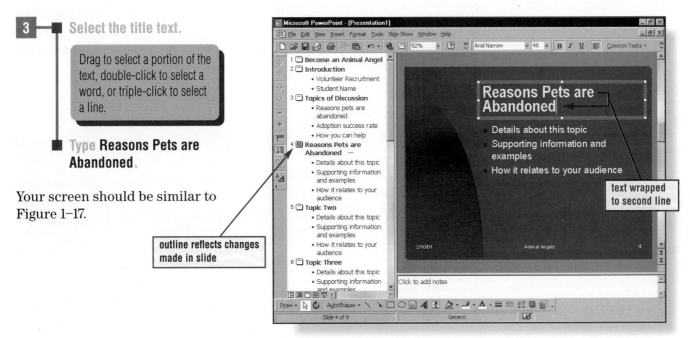

Figure 1–17

Notice the text automatically wrapped to a second line when the length exceeded the width of the box. The Outline pane reflects that changes as they are made in the slide pane. Next you need to replace the sample text in the bulleted list.

4   Click on any of the bulleted items.

Select all three items in the placeholder box.

> Drag to select multiple lines of text, or use Edit/Select All or the shortcut key Ctrl + A to select everything in the placeholder box.

Type **Poor or deteriorating health**.

Press ⏎Enter.

Enter the following text for the next three bullets.

Maintenance expenses
Change in lifestyle
Behavioral problems.

Your screen should be similar to Figure 1–18.

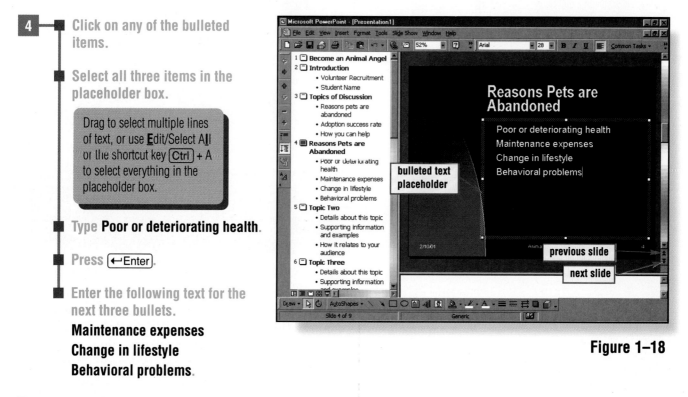

Figure 1–18

Now you are ready to change the text in the next slide. You want this slide to display how the Animal Angels organization helps abandoned pets. In addition to clicking on the slide in the outline pane, the following features can be used to move to other slides in Normal view.

> The ⬆ Previous Slide and ⬇ Next Slide buttons are located at the bottom of the vertical scroll bar.

To Display	Action
Previous slide	Click ⬆
	Click above scroll box
	Press Pg Up
Next slide	Click ⬇
	Click below scroll box
	Press Pg Dn
Any slide	Drag scroll box until the ScreenTip displays the slide you want to view
	Slide: 5 of 9 / Topic Two

You will enter a new slide title and text for the bulleted items.

5 ▪ Display slide 5.

▪ Replace the sample title text with **How Can You Help?**

▪ Select all the text in the bulleted text placeholder.

▪ Type **Donate your time and talent**.

▪ Press ⏎Enter.

You want the next bulleted item to be indented below the first bulleted item. Indenting a bulleted point to the right **demotes** it, or makes it a lower or subordinate topic in the outline hierarchy.

6 ▪ Click ⇨ Demote.

The ⇨ Demote button is on the Formatting and Outlining toolbars.

Your screen should be similar to Figure 1–19.

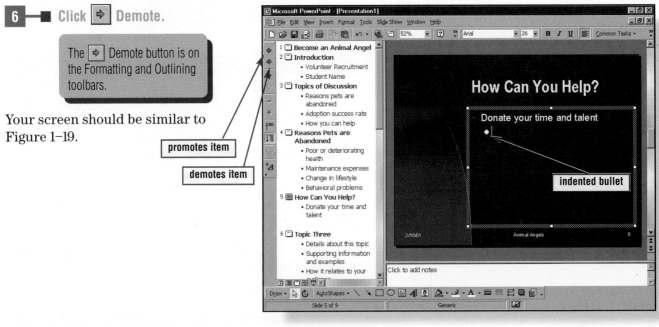

promotes item

demotes item

Figure 1–19

The bullet style of the demoted line has changed to a ◆. When you demote a bulleted point, PowerPoint continues to indent to the same level until you cancel the indent. To enter the next two lines of text,

7 ▪ Type **Become a foster parent**.

▪ Press ⏎Enter.

▪ Type **Work at adoption fairs**.

▪ Press ⏎Enter.

Before entering the next item, you want to remove the indentation, or **promote** the line. Promoting a line moves it to the left, or up a level in the outline hierarchy.

8 — Click ⬅ Promote.

■ Type **Provide financial support**.

■ Press ⏎Enter.

Your screen should be similar to Figure 1–20.

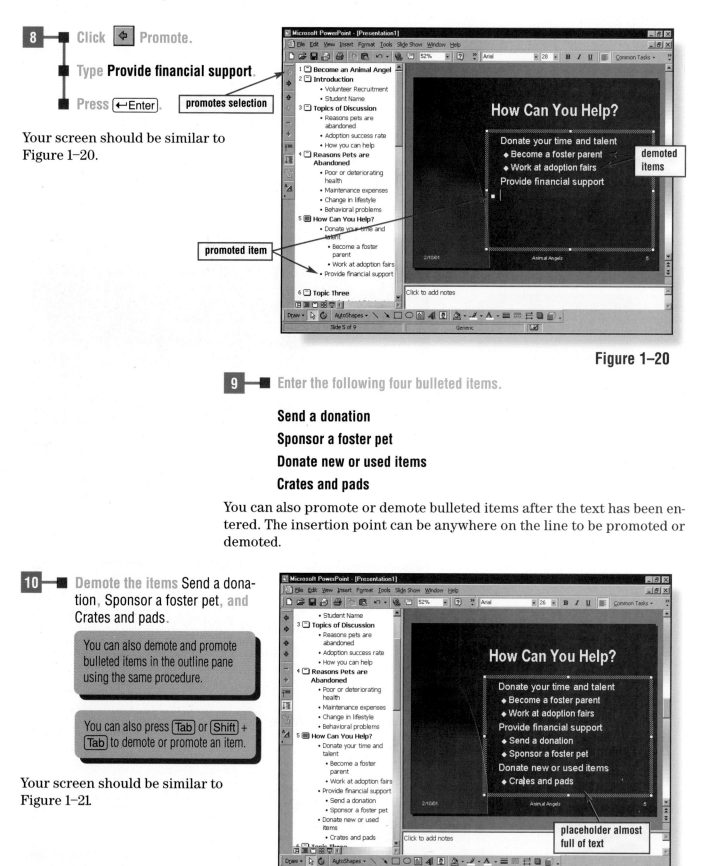

Figure 1–20

9 — Enter the following four bulleted items.

Send a donation

Sponsor a foster pet

Donate new or used items

Crates and pads

You can also promote or demote bulleted items after the text has been entered. The insertion point can be anywhere on the line to be promoted or demoted.

10 — Demote the items Send a donation, Sponsor a foster pet, and Crates and pads.

> You can also demote and promote bulleted items in the outline pane using the same procedure.

> You can also press Tab or Shift + Tab to demote or promote an item.

Your screen should be similar to Figure 1–21.

Figure 1–21

You still have two more bulleted items to add to this text placeholder. Notice, however, that the last item is near the bottom of the box. As you type, PowerPoint's AutoSizing feature will automatically size the text so it fits inside the placeholder. To see how this happens,

11 ■ Move to the end of Crates and pads.

■ Press ←Enter.

■ Type C.

Your screen should be similar to Figure 1–22.

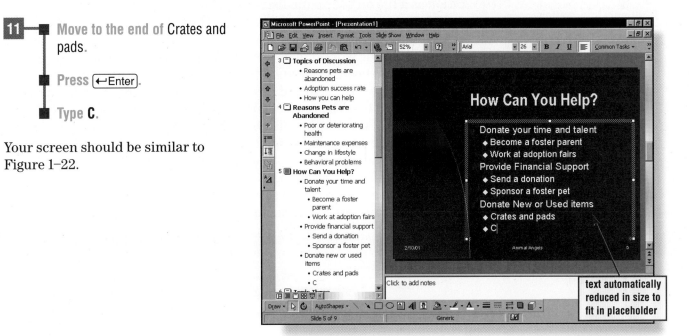

Figure 1–22

Notice how all the text inside the placeholder is reduced so the new text will fit. As you continue entering the last bulleted item, you will see the text size reduced even more.

12 ■ Type ollars and leads.

■ Press ←Enter.

■ Type Food and water bowls.

■ To clear the selection, click outside the placeholder.

Your screen should be similar to Figure 1–23.

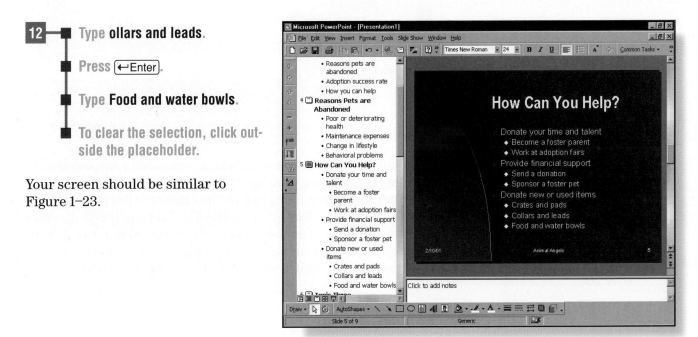

Figure 1–23

Saving the Presentation

You have just been notified of an important meeting that is to begin in a few minutes. Before leaving for the meeting, you want to save the presentation as a file on your data disk.

While working on the presentation, your changes are stored in memory. Not until you save the presentation as a file on a disk are you safe from losing your work due to a power failure or other mishap. When you save a file, you need to specify the location where you want the file stored and a file name. The Save and Save As commands on the File menu can be used to save a file. The Save command saves a presentation by replacing the contents of the existing disk file with the changes you have made, and using the same path and file name as the original document. The Save As command allows you to select the path and provide a different file name. This command lets you save both an original version of a presentation and a revised presentation as two separate files. When a presentation is saved for the first time, either command can be used.

1 Place your data disk in drive A (or the appropriate drive for your system).

Click Save.

> The menu equivalent is **F**ile/**S**ave and the keyboard shortcut is Ctrl + S.

Your screen should be similar to Figure 1–24.

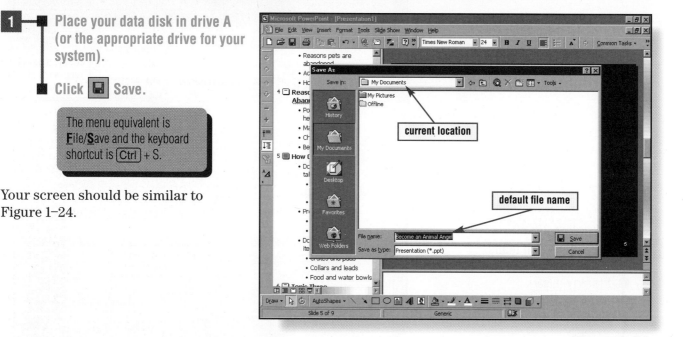

Figure 1–24

The Save As dialog box is displayed in which you specify the location to save the file and the file name. The Save In list box displays the default location where files are stored. The large list box displays the names of any PowerPoint files stored in that location. The File Name text box displays the title from the first slide as the default file name. Notice the default name is highlighted, indicating it is selected and will be replaced as you type the new name. First you will change the file name to Volunteer.

2 ━ ■ Type **Volunteer**.

Your screen should be similar to
Figure 1–25.

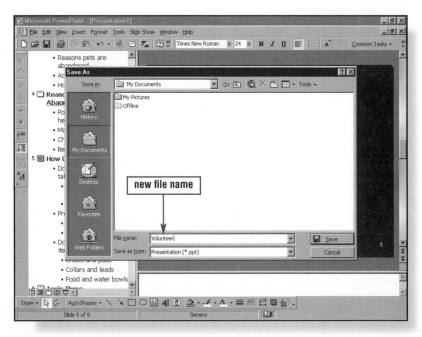

Figure 1–25

The default file name is replaced with new file name. Next you need to
change the location to the drive containing your data disk (A:).

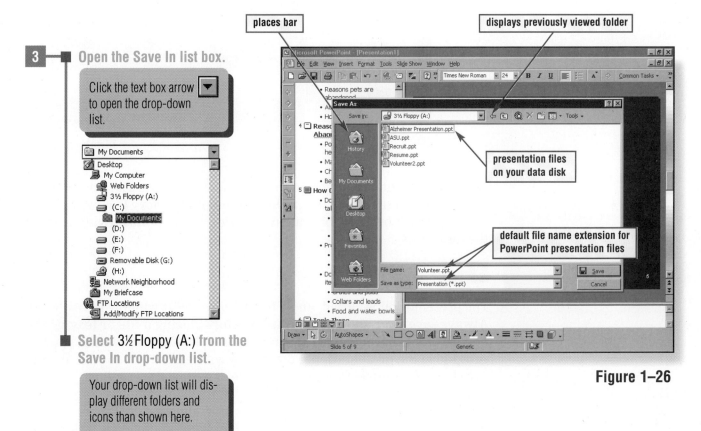

Figure 1–26

3 ━ ■ Open the Save In list box.

> Click the text box arrow ▼
> to open the drop-down
> list.

■ Select 3½ Floppy (A:) from the
Save In drop-down list.

> Your drop-down list will dis-
> play different folders and
> icons than shown here.

Your screen should be similar to
Figure 1–26.

Now the large list box displays the names of all PowerPoint files on your data disk. You can also select the save location from the Places bar along the left side of the dialog box. The icons bring up a list of recently accessed files and folders, the contents of the My Documents and Favorites folders, the Windows desktop, and the remote WebFolders list. Selecting a folder from one of these lists changes to that location. You can also click the ⇐ button in the toolbar to return to folders that were previously opened during the current session.

Notice that the program added the .ppt file extension to the file name. This is the default extension for PowerPoint documents.

If your screen does not display file extensions, your Windows program has this option deactivated.

4 ━ Click 💾 Save

Your screen should be similar to Figure 1–27.

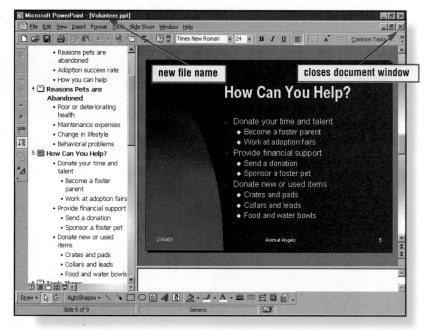

Figure 1–27

The new file name is displayed in the window title bar. The presentation that was on your screen and in the computer's memory is now saved on your data disk in a new file called Volunteer. You are now ready to close the file.

The menu equivalent is **F**ile/**C**lose.

5 ━ Click ☒ Close Window (in the menu bar).

The presentation is closed, and a blank PowerPoint window is displayed. Always save your slide presentation before closing a file or leaving the PowerPoint program. As a safeguard against losing your work if you forget to save the presentation, PowerPoint will remind you to save any unsaved presentation before closing the file or exiting the program.

Note: If you are ending your lab session now, choose **F**ile/E**x**it to exit the program. When you begin again, start PowerPoint and click Cancel to close the startup dialog box.

Opening an Existing Presentation

After returning from your meeting, you hastily continued to enter the information for several more slides. To open this file and see the information in the new slides,

1 ■ Click Open.

> The menu equivalent is **F**ile/**O**pen and the keyboard shortcut is Ctrl + O. You can also select "Open an existing presentation" from the Startup dialog box when PowerPoint is first loaded.

■ If necessary, select drive A (or the drive containing your data disk) from the Look In drop-down list box.

> **Additional Information**
>
> The **F**ile/**N**ew command or the ☐ New button opens a blank new presentation.

Your screen should be similar to Figure 1–28.

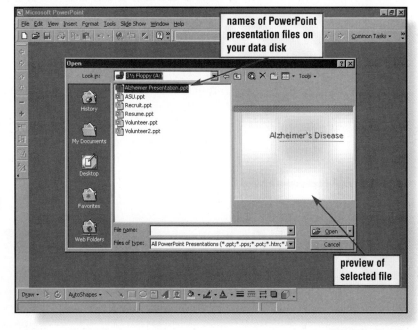

Figure 1–28

> If a preview is not displayed, click ☷ Views and select Pre**v**iew.

From the Open dialog box, you select the location and name of the file you want to open. Because you already specified the location containing your data files, the list box displays the names of all PowerPoint files on your data disk. The first presentation file name is selected, and a preview of the selected file is displayed in the right side of the dialog box.

2 ■ Select Recruit.

■ Click 📂 Open ▾.

> You could also double-click the file name to both select it and choose 📂 Open ▾.

> **Additional Information**
>
> You can also quickly open a recently used file by selecting it from the list of file names displayed at the bottom of the File menu.

Your screen should be similar to Figure 1–29.

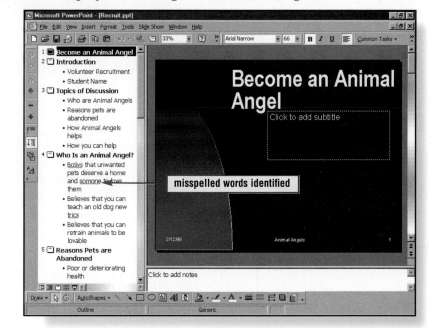

Figure 1–29

3 ━■   Edit slide 2 in the outline pane to display your name.

Checking Spelling Manually

As you entered the information on the additional slides, you left several typing errors uncorrected. To correct the misspelled words and grammatical errors, you can use the shortcut menu to correct each individual word or error, as you learned earlier. However, in many cases you may find it more efficient to wait until you are finished writing before you correct any spelling or grammatical errors. Rather than continually breaking your train of thought to correct errors as you type, you can manually turn on the spelling checker at any time by clicking ⊞ Spell Check or by using the Spelling command on the Tools menu. Another method is to double-click on the spelling indicator ⊞ in the status bar. Using this method moves to the first potential spelling error and displays the shortcut menu.

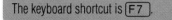
The keyboard shortcut is F7.

1 ━■   Double-click ⊞ in the status box.

Your screen should be similar to Figure 1–30.

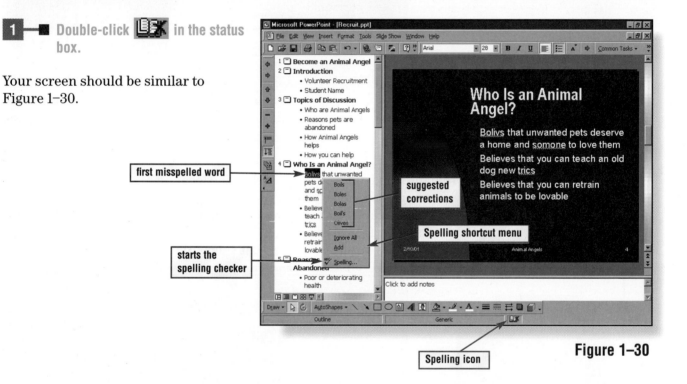

Figure 1–30

The program jumps to slide 4, highlights the first located misspelled word, "Bolivs," in the outline pane, and opens the Spelling shortcut menu. However, the shortcut menu does not display the correct replacement. To see if there are any other suggestions, you will open the Spelling dialog box.

2 ■ Choose Spelling.

Your screen should be similar to Figure 1-31.

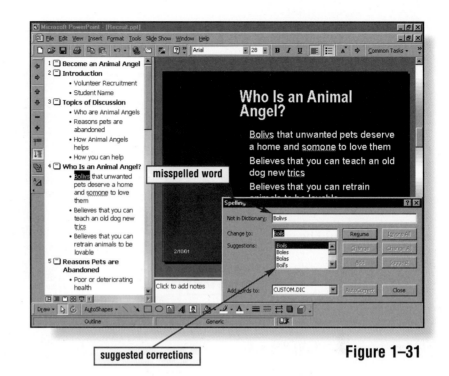

Figure 1-31

Additional Information

The spelling checker identifies many proper names and technical terms as misspelled. To stop this from occurring, use the Add **w**ords option to add those names to your custom dictionary.

The Spelling dialog box displays the misspelled word in the Not in Dictionary text box. The Suggestions list box displays the words the spelling checker has located in the dictionary that most closely match the misspelled word. The first word is highlighted.

3 ■ Scroll the list of suggestions.

Although the list displays several additional suggestions, none of them are correct either. Sometimes the spelling checker does not display any suggested replacements because it cannot locate any words in the dictionaries that are similar in spelling. If there are no suggestions, the Not in Dictionary text box simply displays the word that is highlighted in the text. Because none of the suggestions is correct, you need to edit the word yourself by typing the correction in the Change to text box.

4 Type **Believes** in the Change To text box.

Click [Change].

Additional Information

You can also edit words directly in the presentation and then click [Resume] to continue checking spelling.

Your screen should be similar to Figure 1–32.

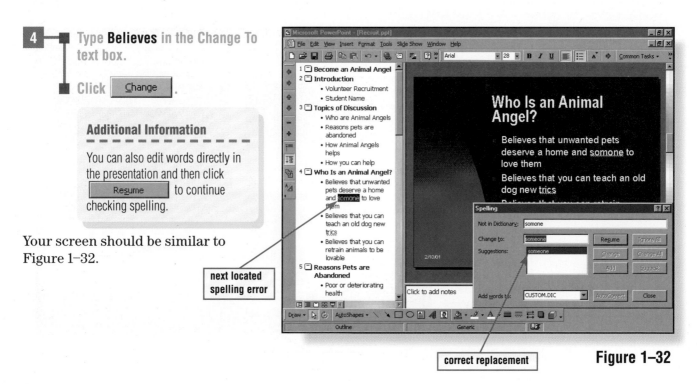

Figure 1–32

Once the Spelling dialog box is open, the spelling checker continues to check the entire presentation for spelling errors. The next misspelled word, "somone," is identified. In this case, the suggested replacement is correct.

If necessary, move the dialog box to see the located misspelled word.

5 Click [Change].

The next misspelled word is identified, and "tricks" is the correct replacement.

6 Click [Change].

There should be no other misspelled words. However, if the spelling checker encounters others in your file, correct them as needed. When no others are located, PowerPoint will display a message box telling you that spell-check has finished. To close the message box,

7 Click [OK].

Deleting Slides

To get a better overall picture of all slides in the presentation, you will switch to Slide Sorter view.

1 ■ Click ⊞ Slide Sorter view.

> The menu equivalent is **V**iew/Sli**d**e Sorter.

Your screen should be similar to Figure 1–33.

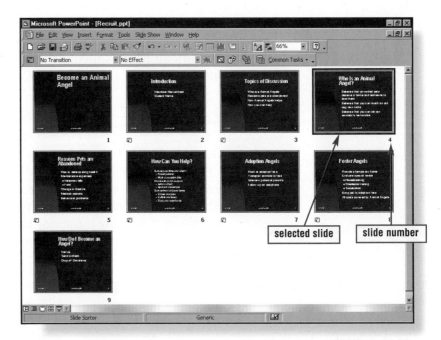

Figure 1–33

Viewing the slides side by side helps you see how your presentation flows. There are still nine slides in the presentation, but all the sample text that was provided by the AutoContent Wizard has been replaced by the text for the presentation. The slide number appears below each slide. Notice that slide 4, the slide you were last viewing in Slide view, is displayed with a dark border around it. This indicates that the slide is selected. As you look at the slides, you decide the second slide does not really add much to the presentation and you want to delete it.

2 ■ Select slide 2.

> Clicking on a slide selects it.

■ Press Delete.

> The menu equivalent is **E**dit/**D**elete Slide.

Your screen should be similar to Figure 1–34.

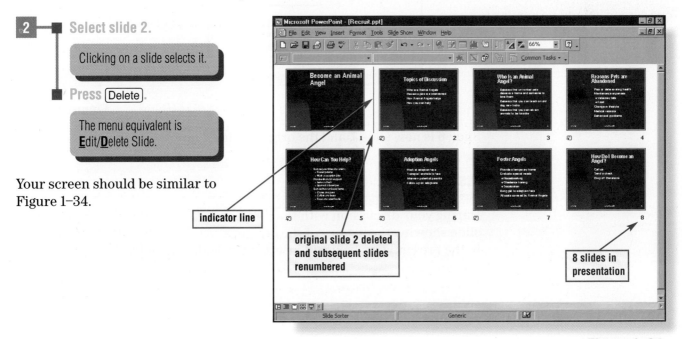

Figure 1–34

The Introduction slide has been deleted, and slides 3 through 9 have been appropriately renumbered. There are now eight slides in the presentation. An indicator line appears between slides 1 and 2 where the deleted slide once existed.

Moving Slides

Next you decide to switch the order of slide 6, Adoption Angels, with slide 7, Foster Angels. To reorder a slide in Slide Sorter view, you drag it to its new location using drag and drop. As you drag the mouse pointer, the indicator line appears to show you where the slide will appear in the presentation. When the indicator line is located where you want the slide to be placed, release the mouse button.

1 ▪ Select slide 6.

▪ Drag the mouse pointer until the indicator line is displayed after slide 7.

▪ Release the mouse button.

> You can also use the Cut and Paste commands on the Edit menu to move slides in Slide Sorter view.

Your screen should be similar to Figure 1–35.

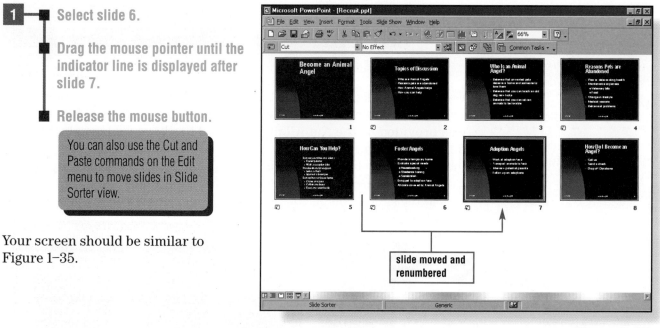

Figure 1–35

Slide 6 is now slide 7, and the original slide 7 is now slide 6.

Inserting a Slide

During your discussion with the director, it was suggested that you add a slide showing the history of the organization. To include this information in the presentation, you will insert a new slide after slide 2.

1 Click in the space between slide 2 and slide 3.

> The indicator line shows you where the new slide will be added.

Click 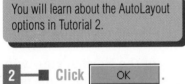 New Slide.

> If the New Slide dialog box is not displayed, delete the new slide and turn on this feature using **T**ools/**O**ptions/View/**N**ew slide dialog.

> The menu equivalent is **I**nsert/**N**ew Slide and the keyboard shortcut is Ctrl + M.

Your screen should be similar to Figure 1–36.

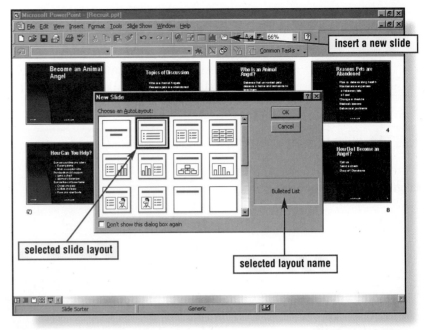

insert a new slide

selected slide layout

selected layout name

Figure 1–36

> You will learn about the AutoLayout options in Tutorial 2.

From the New Slide dialog box you need to select the layout for the new slide. The default layout, Bulleted List, is selected. To accept the default and insert the slide,

2 Click OK .

Your screen should be similar to Figure 1–37.

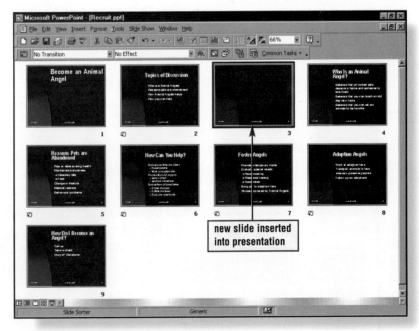

new slide inserted into presentation

Figure 1–37

Setting and Using Tabs

Next you will add text to the slide presenting a brief history of the Animal Angels organization. You will enter the text in Slide view. The enlarged slide pane of this view makes it easier to see some formatting changes as they occur on the slide.

1 ■ Click ▭ to switch to Slide view.

Your screen should be similar to Figure 1–38.

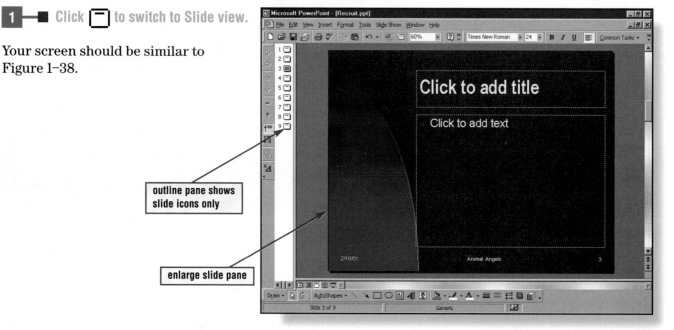

Figure 1–38

This view is the same as the slide pane portion of the Normal view window. The notes pane, however, is not displayed, and the outline pane is reduced to a list of slide icons. First you will enter the slide title and then a list of dates and events. You do not want the list bulleted, however, so you will turn off this feature.

2 ■ Click in the title placeholder.

■ Type **Animal Angels History**.

■ Click in the text placeholder.

■ Click ▤ Bullets to turn off bullets.

> The menu equivalent to turn off/on bulleted lists is F**o**rmat/**B**ullets and Numbering/Bulleted/None or select a bullet style.

■ Use **V**iew/**R**uler to display the ruler if the ruler is not already displayed.

Your screen should be similar to Figure 1–39.

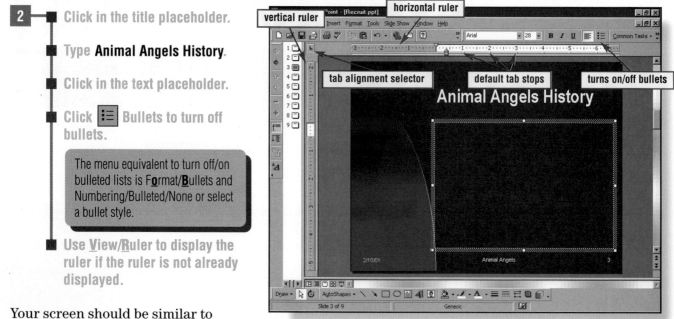

Figure 1–39

The horizontal and vertical rulers are used to position objects precisely on the slide and to adjust indents and tabs in text.

You will enter the list of dates and events shown below.

Year	Event
1990	Founded by Ed Wilton
1991	Built first shelter
1996	Began volunteer program
1999	Expanded to 10 shelters

To make it easier to align the two columns, you will set tab stops. A **tab stop** is a stopping point along a line to which text will indent when you press Tab. You can select from four different types of tab stops that control how characters are positioned or aligned with the tab stop. The four tab types, the alignment tab mark that appears on the ruler, and the effects on the text are explained in the following table.

Alignment	Tab Mark	How It Affects Text	Example
Left	⌊L⌋	Extends text to right from tab stop	left
Center	⌊⊥⌋	Aligns text centered on tab	center
Right	⌊⌟⌋	Extends text to left from tab stop	right
Decimal	⌊⊥⌋	Aligns text with decimal point	35.78

Setting different types of tab stops is helpful for aligning text or numeric data vertically in columns. Using tab stops ensures that the text will indent to the same set location. Setting tab stops instead of pressing Tab or Spacebar repeatedly is a more professional way to format a document, as well as faster and more accurate.

You can quickly specify tab stop locations and types using the ruler. To select a tab stop type, click the ⌊L⌋ tab alignment selector box on the left end of the ruler to cycle through the types. Then to specify where to place the selected tab stop type, click on the location in the ruler. Drag any tab marker to a new position or off the ruler to remove it. You will add a left tab stop at the .5 inch and 1.5 inch positions.

3 — Click the .5 position on the ruler.

The default tab type is Left and should already be selected in the tab alignment selector box.

■ Click the 1.5 position on the ruler.

■ Press [Tab] once.

■ Type **Year**.

■ Press [Tab].

■ Type **Event**.

■ Press [Enter].

Your screen should be similar to Figure 1–40.

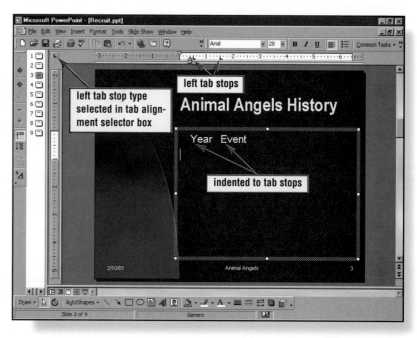

Figure 1–40

4 — Continue entering the information shown below. Remember to press [Tab] to create the columns.

1990 Founded by Ed Wilton

1991 Built first shelter

1996 Began volunteer program

1999 Expanded to 10 shelters

■ Use <u>V</u>iew/<u>R</u>uler to turn off the ruler display.

Your screen should be similar to Figure 1–41.

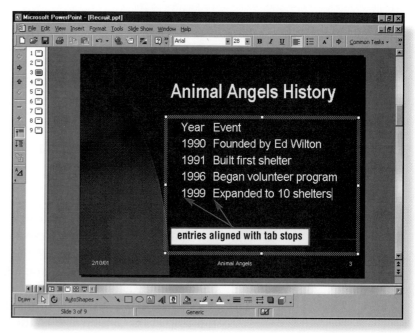

Figure 1–41

Rehearsing a Presentation

Now that the slides are in the order you want, you would like to see how the presentation will look when viewed by an audience. A simple way to rehearse a presentation is to view it electronically as a slide show. While the slide show is running, you can plan what you want to say to supplement the information provided on the slides.

A **slide show** is an onscreen display of your presentation. Each slide fills the screen, hiding the PowerPoint application window, so you can view the slides as your audience would. To begin the slide show starting with the first slide,

1 ▪ Select slide 1 in the outline pane.

▪ Click 🖵 Slide Show.

The menu equivalent is **V**iew/Slide Sho**w** and the keyboard shortcut is F5 .

Your screen should be similar to Figure 1–42.

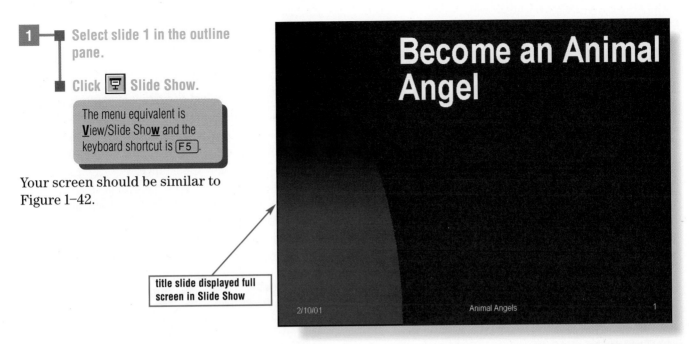

title slide displayed full screen in Slide Show

Figure 1–42

The presentation title slide is displayed full screen as it will appear when projected on a screen using computer projection equipment. The easiest way to see the next slide is to click the mouse button. You could also press Spacebar , Enter , → , ↓ , or Page Down , or select Next from the shortcut menu or type the letter "N" (for Next).

2 ▪ Click to display the next slide.

▪ Using each of the methods described, slowly display the entire presentation.

The last slide displays a black window, indicating the end of the slide show has been reached. After the last slide is displayed, the program returns to the view you were last using, in this case Slide view.

Enhancing the Presentation

While looking at the slide show, you decide that the title slide needs to have more impact. To do this, you will change the look of the title text and add a picture to the slide. You also realize you need to add your name to the title slide.

Changing Fonts and Font Size

First you will improve the appearance of the presentation title by changing the font design of the title text.

Concept ⑥ **Fonts**

A **font** is a set of characters with a specific design. Using fonts as a design element can add interest to your presentation. The designs have names such as Times New Roman and Arial. Some fonts such as Times New Roman are very traditional and are best for a serious presentation. Others, such as Comic Sans MS are more fun and are best used in a lighthearted presentation. It is also a good idea to use no more than three to four different fonts in a presentation so that the presentation has a consistent appearance.

There are two basic types of fonts, serif and sans serif. **Serif fonts** have a flair at the base of each letter that visually leads the reader to the next letter. Serif fonts generally are for the main part of your presentation as they are easy to read. **Sans serif fonts** do not have a flair at the base of each letter. Because sans serif fonts have a clean look, they generally are used for headings to grab the audience's attention.

Each font has one or more sizes. **Font size** is the height of the character and is commonly measured in **points**, abbreviated "pt." One point equals about 1/72 inch, and text in most presentations starts at 24 points. For headings on your slides, you should use a size of 48 to 60 points. Some common fonts in different sizes are shown below.

This is Arial 12 pt.

This is Arial 24 pt.

This is Arial 36 pt.

This is Times New Roman 12 pt.

This is Times New Roman 24 pt.

This is Times New Roman 36 pt.

To change the font before typing the text, use the command and then type. All text will appear in the specified font setting until another font setting is selected. To change a font setting for existing text, select the text you want to change and then use the command. You will change the font of the title to Comic Sans MS.

1 Select the text Become an Animal Angel.

Open the `Arial Narrow` Font drop-down list.

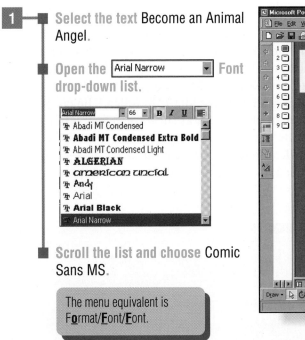

Scroll the list and choose Comic Sans MS.

The menu equivalent is F**o**rmat/**F**ont/**F**ont.

Your screen should be similar to Figure 1–43.

Figure 1–43

The text has changed to the new font style and the Font button displays the font name used in the current selection. But it is a little larger than you want it to be. To reduce it,

2 Click A˅ Decrease Font Size twice.

Use A˄ Increase Font Size to incrementally increase the point size of selected text.

You could also specify the point size from the `24` Font Size drop-down list or use F**o**rmat/**F**ont/**S**ize.

Your screen should be similar to Figure 1–44.

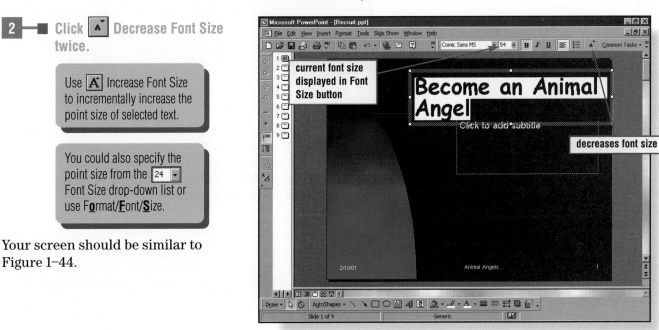

Figure 1–44

Additional Information

If a selection includes text in several different sizes, the smallest size would appear in the Font Size button followed by a + sign.

The Font Size button displays the point size of the current selection.

Sizing and Moving a Placeholder

Even though you have reduced the point size, the title text still wraps to a second line because it is larger than the width of the placeholder. To fix this you will adjust the size of the placeholder.

To adjust the placeholder size, drag the sizing handles. The corner handles will adjust both the height and width at the same time, whereas the center handles adjust the side borders to which they are associated. When you point to the sizing handle, the mouse pointer appears as ←→, indicating the direction you can drag to adjust the size. The placeholder needs to be longer only.

1 ■ Point to the left center handle and drag to the left until the text appears on a single line.

Your screen should be similar to Figure 1–45.

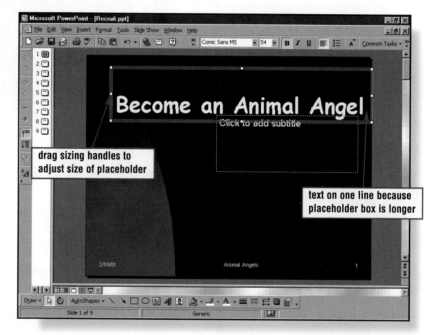

Figure 1–45

Next you want to move the placeholder up slightly. An object can be moved anywhere on a slide, including right up to the very edge. A placeholder is moved by dragging the selection rectangle. The mouse pointer appears as ✛ when you can move a placeholder. A dotted outline is displayed as you drag the placeholder to show your new location.

2 ▪ Point to the selection rectangle (not a handle) and drag the title to its new location (use Figure 1–46 as a reference).

▪ Clear the selection.

Your screen should be similar to Figure 1–46.

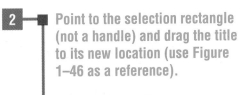

Figure 1–46

3 ▪ Enter your name in the subtitle placeholder.

▪ Reduce the size of the subtitle placeholder to fit the contents.

▪ Move the subtitle placeholder to the lower right corner of the slide.

Inserting a Picture

Next, you want to add a picture of one of the pets that is up for adoption to the title slide. A picture is one of several different graphic objects that can be added to a slide.

Concept ⑦ Graphics

A **graphic** is an object such as a drawing or picture that can be added to a slide. A graphic can be a simple **drawing object,** consisting of shapes such as lines and boxes, that can be created using features on the Drawing toolbar. A **picture** is an illustration such as a scanned photograph. It is a graphic that was created from another program. Many pictures can be edited using the features in the Picture toolbar.

We are
pleased to
announce
the grand
opening of
Toms Deli

Picture files can be obtained from a variety of sources. Many simple drawings called **clip art** are available in the Clip Gallery that comes with Office 2000. You can also create graphic files using a scanner to convert any printed document, including photographs, to an electronic format. Most images that are scanned and inserted into documents are stored as Windows bitmap files (.bmp). All types of graphics, including clip art, photographs, and other types of images, can be found on the Internet. These files are commonly stored as .jpg or .pcx files. Keep in mind that any images you locate on the Internet may be protected by copyright and should only be used with permission. You can also purchase CD's containing graphics for your use.

Add graphics to your presentation to help the reader understand concepts, to add interest, and to make your presentation stand out from others.

Additional Information

You can also scan a picture and insert it directly into a slide without saving it as a file first.

You recently scanned a photograph of a puppy that is looking for a new home and saved it as Puppy.jpg. You will add the picture to the slide below the title.

1 ■ Choose Insert/Picture.

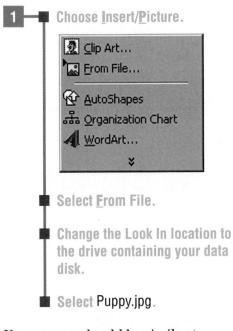

■ Select From File.

■ Change the Look In location to the drive containing your data disk.

■ Select Puppy.jpg.

Your screen should be similar to Figure 1–47.

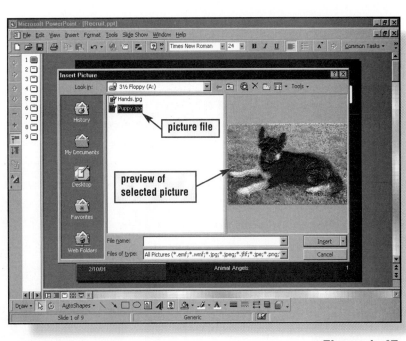

Figure 1–47

If a preview is not displayed, click ▦ Views and select Preview.

The Insert Picture dialog box is similar to the Open File and Save File dialog boxes, except the only types of files listed are files with picture file extensions. A preview of the picture appears to the right of the list.

2 ■ Click Insert ▾.

Your screen should be similar to Figure 1–48.

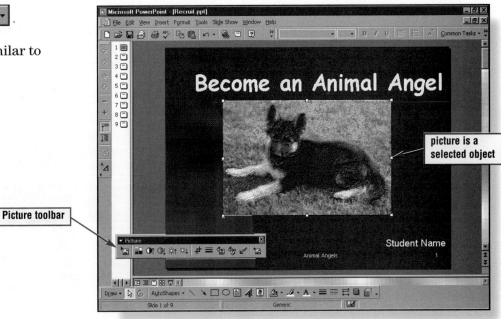

Figure 1–48

The picture is surrounded by sizing handles, indicating it is a selected object. Frequently, when a graphic is inserted, its size will need to be adjusted. A graphic object is sized and moved just like a placeholder. You want to reduce the picture size slightly and position it in the space below the title. The Picture toolbar is used to modify the selected picture object.

3 ▪ Reduce the size of the picture object slightly and position it as shown in Figure 1–49.

▪ Clear the selection.

Your screen should be similar to Figure 1–49.

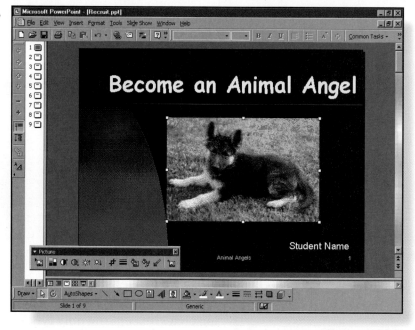

Figure 1–49

Inserting Clip Art

Finally, you think a "picture frame" effect around the picture would set it off better. Among the many clip art graphics included with Office 2000 are several that can be used as borders and frames around objects.

1 ▪ Click 🖼 Insert Clip Art (in the Drawing toolbar).

> The menu equivalent is Insert/Picture/Clip Art.

▪ If necessary, open the Pictures tab.

Your screen should be similar to Figure 1–50.

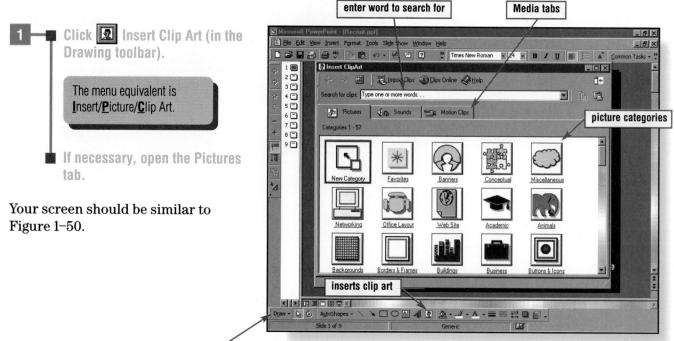

Figure 1–50

The categories and images in your dialog box may be different from those in Figure 1–50.

The Insert ClipArt dialog box Media tabs organize the different media by type. The Pictures tab displays the Clip Gallery containing clip art, photographs, scanned images, drawings, and other graphics. Sound effects and music files are in the Sounds tab, and videos and animation files are in the Motion Clips tab.

Each clip art image has been named and assigned several keywords that describe the content of the image. The images are then stored under the different categories to help make it easy for you to locate. Many clip art images are in multiple categories. You can click on a category and look for the graphic you want to use, or you can quickly locate clip art by entering a keyword in the Search for Clips text box. You will search using a keyword.

2 ■ In the Search for Clips text box, type **frame**.

■ Press (←Enter).

Your screen should be similar to Figure 1–51.

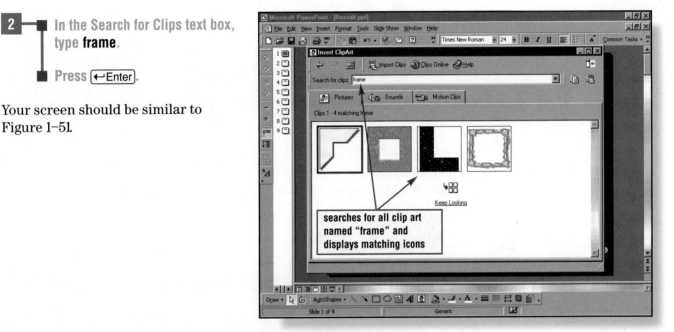

Figure 1–51

After a few moments, icons of all clip art images that have "frame" in their description are displayed. Pointing to an image displays the image name in a ScreenTip. You want to insert the clip art named "frame."

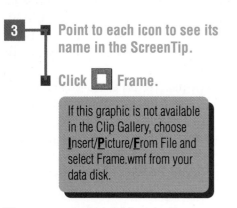

3 ► Point to each icon to see its name in the ScreenTip.

■ Click ☐ Frame.

If this graphic is not available in the Clip Gallery, choose **I**nsert/**P**icture/**F**rom File and select Frame.wmf from your data disk.

Your screen should be similar to Figure 1–52.

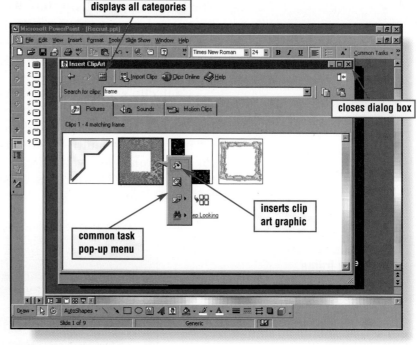

displays all categories

closes dialog box

inserts clip art graphic

common task pop-up menu

Figure 1–52

A pop-up menu of common tasks appears. With the icons on this toolbar, you can insert the clip, preview the clip in a larger size, add the clip to your list of Favorites, or find other clips that are similar. To insert the selected graphic,

4 ► Click ☒ Insert Clip.

■ Click ☷ All Categories to display the category list again.

■ Click ☒ to close the dialog box.

Your screen should be similar to Figure 1–53.

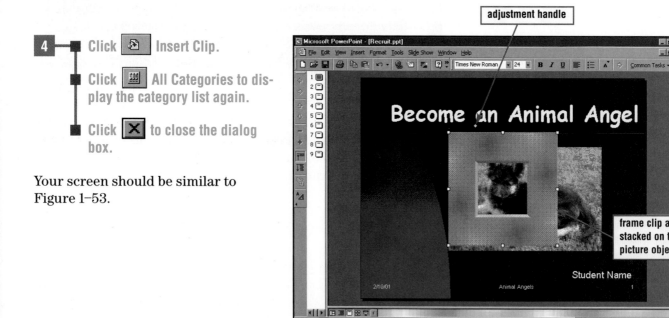

adjustment handle

Become an Animal Angel

frame clip art stacked on top of picture object

Figure 1–53

Additional Information

To change the stacking order, open the Dr**a**w button menu on the Drawing toolbar and select O**r**der .

The clip art image is inserted in the slide. It appears on top of the picture object. As objects are added to a slide, they automatically stack in individual layers. Since the frame was the last object added to the slide, it is on the top layer of the stack. You can bring an object forward or backward in the stack or directly to the top or bottom of the stack.

Next you want to size the frame to surround the picture. Notice in addition to the sizing handles, a yellow diamond adjustment handle is displayed. This handle is used to adjust the appearance, not the size of the object. Using the adjustment handle on the frame will adjust the width of the border. You need to increase the outside dimension of the frame as well as make the frame border narrower to display more of the picture inside the frame.

5 ■ Move the frame object so it is centered over the picture.

■ Drag the corner sizing handles until the outside of the frame overlaps the edge of the puppy picture.

■ Drag the adjustment handle outward until the puppy is fully visible inside the frame.

■ Continue to adjust the size and position of the frame as needed until it appears as in Figure 1–54.

Your screen should be similar to Figure 1–54.

Figure 1–54

Now you think the title slide will make a much better impression. To see how the changes and enhancements you have made to the presentation will look full screen, you will run the slide show again.

6 ■ Run the slide show from the first slide.

Previewing the Presentation in Black and White

Although your presentation is in color, you want to print a black-and-white copy of the slides for the agency director to review. Shading, patterns, and backgrounds that look good on the screen can make printed handouts unreadable, so you want to preview how the printout will look in black and white before making a copy for the director.

The menu equivalent is **V**iew/**B**lack and White.

Your screen should be similar to Figure 1–55.

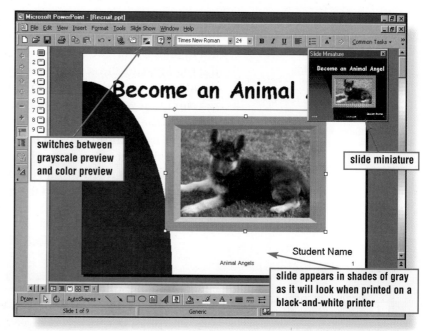

Figure 1–55

Use **V**iew/Slide M**i**niature to display a color miniature.

The slide is displayed using the default black-and-white options. A small color miniature of the slide may also be displayed if this feature is on. The default settings display the background white, text black, and patterns in grayscale. Grayscale displays shades of gray to represent colors and shadings. The default settings can be changed to improve the appearance of the printed slides.

2 To see these options, display the slide shortcut menu and point to Black and White.

The Black and White submenu options are used to select different variations of the black-and-white slide. The default setting, White, creates a black-and-white slide using shades of gray and black on a white background. You like how the black-and-white version of your presentation looks.

3 Click anywhere in the workspace to cancel the menu.

Click Grayscale Preview.

The slide is displayed in color again.

Saving an Existing Presentation

Now you are ready to save the changes you have made to the file on your data disk using the Save or Save As commands on the File menu. Because you may want to redo this tutorial and use the file again, you will use the Save As command to save your edited version using a new file name.

1 ■ Choose **File/Save As**.

The file name of the file you opened, Recruit, is displayed in the File Name text box of the Save As dialog box. To save the document as Recruit1, you can type the new file name entirely, or you can edit the existing name. In this case, it is easier to edit the file name by adding the number to the end of the name.

2 ■ Click at the end of the file name before the period.

> If you do not clear the highlight, the selected file name will be cleared and replaced with the new text as it is typed.

■ Type **1**.

■ Click  .

The new file name, Recruit1, is displayed in the window title bar. The original document file is unchanged on your data disk. The view that is displayed when the file is saved is the view in which it will be displayed when opened.

Printing a Presentation

Although you still plan to make several changes to the presentation, you want to give a printed copy of the presentation to the agency director to get feedback regarding the content and layout. To print the presentation,

1 ■ Choose **File/Print**.

> The keyboard shortcut is Ctrl + P. You can use the 🖨 Print button if you do not need to make any changes to the default print settings.

Your screen should be similar to Figure 1–56.

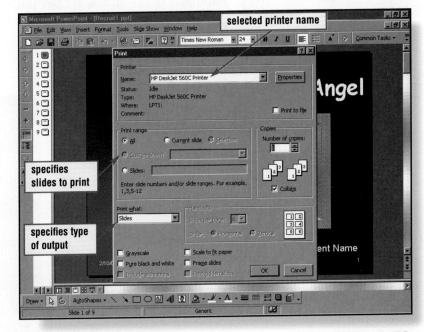

Figure 1–56

The Name text box in the Printer section displays the name of the selected printer. You may need to specify the printer you will be using. (Your instructor will provide the printer to select).

2 ▬ If you need to select a different printer, open the Name drop-down list and select the appropriate printer.

The Print Range settings specify which slides to print. The default setting, All, prints all the slides, while Current Slide prints only the slide you are viewing. The Slides option is used to specify specific slides or a range of slides to print by entering the slide numbers in the text box. The Copies section is used to specify the number of copies of the specified print range. The default is to print one copy.

The Print What option is used to specify the type of presentation document you want to print: slides, handouts, outlines, or note pages. PowerPoint can print only one type of output at a time. The default is slides. The output types are described in the table below.

Output type	Description
Slides	Prints one slide per page
Handouts	Prints multiple slides per page
Outline View	Prints the slide content as it appears in Outline view
Notes pages	Prints the slide and the associated notes on a page

> You will learn about notes in Tutorial 2.

> The Pure Black and White option prints your presentation in pure black and white, which hides all shades of gray.

At the bottom of the dialog box, PowerPoint displays options that allow you to print color slides as black-and-white slides, to make the slide images fill the paper, and to add a frame around the slide. If you have a black-and-white printer, grayscale slides are printed by default. You will print handouts of the slides, six per page in grayscale.

3 ▬ Open the Print What drop-down list.

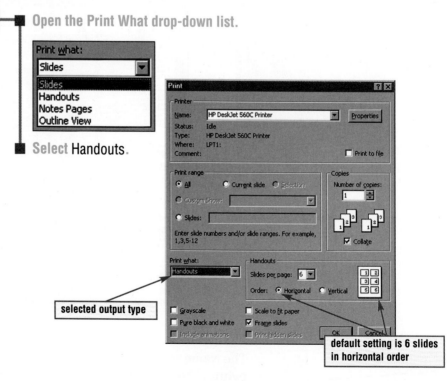

▬ Select Handouts.

selected output type

default setting is 6 slides in horizontal order

The Handouts section of the dialog box is now activated. You can now specify the number of slides per page to print and the order. The default of 6 in horizontal order is appropriate.

4 ■ Select Grayscale.

■ Click OK.

The  Printer icon appears in the status bar, indicating that the program is sending data to the Print Manager. Your handouts should be printing.

Exiting PowerPoint

You will continue to work on the presentation in the next tutorial. If you are ready to exit the PowerPoint program,

1 ■ Choose File/Exit.

■ If asked to save the file again, choose No.

Concept Summary

Tutorial 1: Creating a Presentation

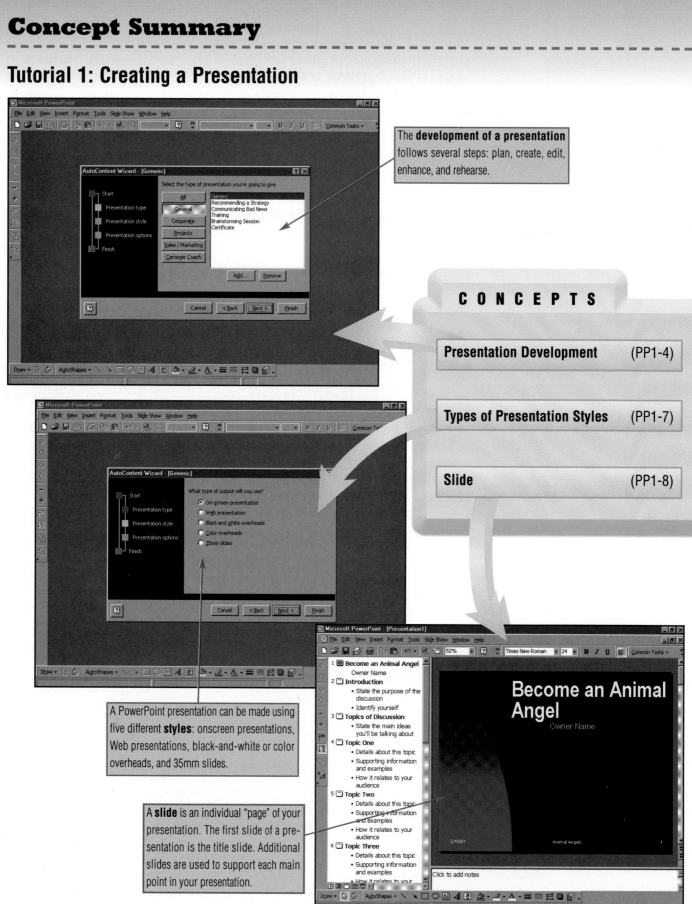

The **development of a presentation** follows several steps: plan, create, edit, enhance, and rehearse.

CONCEPTS

Presentation Development   (PP1-4)

Types of Presentation Styles   (PP1-7)

Slide   (PP1-8)

A PowerPoint presentation can be made using five different **styles**: onscreen presentations, Web presentations, black-and-white or color overheads, and 35mm slides.

A **slide** is an individual "page" of your presentation. The first slide of a presentation is the title slide. Additional slides are used to support each main point in your presentation.

The **AutoCorrect** feature makes some basic assumptions about the text you are typing and, based on these assumptions, automatically identifies and/or corrects the entry.

The **automatic spelling checker** feature advises you of misspelled words as you create and edit a presentation, and proposes possible corrections.

A **font** is a set of characters with a specific design. Using fonts as a design element can add interest to your presentation.

AutoCorrect	(PP1-13)
Automatic spelling checker	(PP1-13)
Fonts	(PP1-36)
Graphics	(PP1-40)

A **graphic** is an object such as a drawing or picture that can be added to a slide.

Tutorial Review

Key Terms

AutoContent Wizard   PP1-4
AutoCorrect   PP1-13
clip art   PP1-40
custom dictionary   PP1-13
demote   PP1-19
design template   PP1-4
drawing object   PP1-40
Drawing toolbar   PP1-3
font   PP1-36
font size   PP1-36
footer   PP1-8

Formatting toolbar   PP1-3
graphic   PP1-40
main dictionary   PP1-13
object   PP1-16
Outlining toolbar   PP1-3
pane   PP1-9
picture   PP1-40
placeholder   PP1-16
point   PP1-36
promote   PP1-19
sans serif font   PP1-36

selection handles   PP1-17
selection rectangle   PP1-17
serif font   PP1-36
sizing handles   PP1-17
slide   PP1-8
slide show   PP1-34
Standard toolbar   PP1-3
tab stop   PP1-33
view   PP1-9
workspace   PP1-3

Command Summary

Command	Shortcut Keys	Button	Action
File/New	Ctrl + N		Creates new presentation
File/Open	Ctrl + O		Opens selected presentation
File/Close			Closes presentation
File/Save	Ctrl + S		Saves presentation
File/Save As			Saves presentation using new file name
File/Print	Ctrl + P		Prints presentation using default print settings
File/Exit			Exits PowerPoint program
Edit/Undo	Ctrl + Z		Reverses the last action
Edit/Select All	Ctrl + A		Selects all objects on a slide or all text in an object, or (in Outline pane) an entire outline
Edit/Delete Slide	Delete		Deletes selected slide
View/Normal			Switches to Normal view
View/Slide Sorter			Switches to Slide Sorter view
View/Slide Show	F5		Runs slide show
View/Black and White			Displays slides in black and white

Command	Shortcut Keys	Button	Action
View/Slide M**i**niature			Displays or hides miniature version of the slide
View/**R**uler			Displays/hides vertical and horizontal rulers
Insert/**N**ew Slide	Ctrl + M		Inserts new slide
Insert/**P**icture/**C**lip Art			Opens Clip Gallery and inserts selected clip art
Insert/**P**icture/**F**rom File			Inserts a picture from file on disk
F**o**rmat/**F**ont/**F**ont		Arial Narrow	Changes font type
F**o**rmat/**F**ont/**S**ize		A A 24	Changes font size
Tools/**S**pelling	F7		Spell-checks presentation
Tools/**O**ptions/View/**N**ew slide dialog			Turns on/off display of the New Slide dialog box
D**r**aw/O**r**der			Changes stacking order of drawing objects

Screen Identification

1. In the following PowerPoint screen, several items are identified by letters. Enter the correct term for each item in the spaces that follow.

a. _____

b. _____

c. _____

d. _____

e. _____

f. _____

g. _____

h. _____

i. _____

j. _____

k. _____

l. _____

m. _____

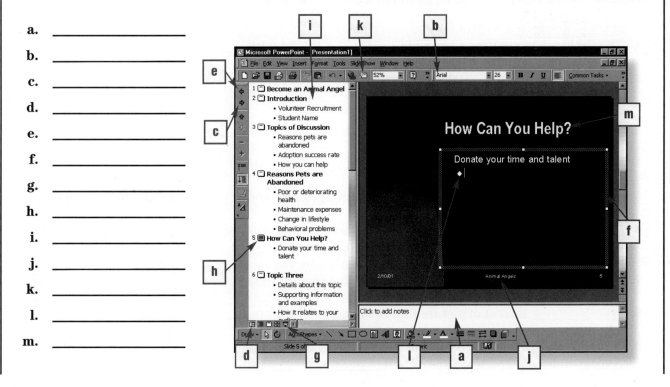

Matching

Match the numbered item with the correct lettered description.

1. AutoContent Wizard _____ a. displays enlarged slide pane and reduced outline pane

2. Slide view _____ b. displays a miniature of each slide

3. placeholder _____ c. guides you through steps to create a presentation

4. selection rectangle _____ d. prints multiple slides per page

5. demote _____ e. indents bulleted item

6. .ppt _____ f. displays each slide using the full screen space in final form

7. Slide Sorter view _____ g. used to change the size of a placeholder

8. slide show _____ h. boxes that contain specific types of items or objects

9. handle _____ i. default extension for PowerPoint documents

10. handouts _____ j. allows text entry, deletion, selection, and formatting when border appears hatched

Fill-In

Complete the following statements by filling in the blanks with the correct terms.

1. The first step in creating a presentation is to understand its _____.

2. Practicing or _____ the delivery of your presentation is the final step in presentation development.

3. When selected, the title placeholder is surrounded with eight _____.

4. A _____ is an individual "page" of your presentation.

5. In _____ view, the slide pane is enlarged so you can work on enhancing the slides.

6. _____ is a PowerPoint feature that advises you of misspelled words as you create and edit a document and proposes possible corrections.

7. _____ is a set of characters with a specific design.

8. _____ is a set of picture files or simple drawings that comes with Office 2000.

9. Boxes that are designed to contain specific types of objects such as the slide title, bulleted text, charts, tables, and pictures are called _____.

10. A _____ is text or graphics that appears at the bottom of each slide.

Multiple Choice

1. The large area of the screen where presentations are displayed is called the _____.

   a. work area
   b. workspace
   c. window pane
   d. document area

2. The step in the development of a presentation that focuses on grabbing and holding the audience's attention is _____.

   a. plan
   b. create
   c. edit
   d. enhance

3. PowerPoint can be used to create _____.

   a. onscreen presentations
   b. Web presentations
   c. black-and-white or color overheads
   d. all the above

4. The first slide of a presentation is the _____ slide.

   a. summary
   b. title
   c. support
   d. introduction

5. _____ view contains three separate panes so that you can work on all aspects of your presentation.

   a. Slide Sorter
   b. Normal
   c. Slide
   d. Outline

6. When the Spelling Checker is used, words are checked against the _____ dictionary first.

   a. custom
   b. official
   c. main
   d. common

7. Boxes that contain objects such as the slide title, bulleted text, charts, tables, and pictures are called _____.

   a. placeholders
   b. dialogs
   c. forms
   d. slides

8. A(n) _____ is an onscreen display of your presentation.

   a. outline
   b. handout
   c. slide show
   d. slide

9. _____ fonts have a flair at the base of each letter that visually leads the reader to the next letter.

   a. sans serif
   b. serif
   c. printer
   d. display

10. Objects such as charts, drawings, pictures, and scanned photographs that provide visual interest or clarify data are _____.

   a. drawing objects
   b. clip art
   c. graphics
   d. none of the above

True/False

Circle the correct answer to the following questions.

1.	The AutoContent Wizard is a guided approach that helps you determine the content and organization of your presentation through a series of questions.	True	False
2.	PowerPoint provides six different views that are used to look at and modify your presentation.	True	False
3.	The Drawing toolbar contains buttons that are used to change the appearance or format of the document.	True	False
4.	Onscreen presentations can be designed specifically for the World Wide Web, where a browser serves as the presentation tool.	True	False
5.	A selected title placeholder is surrounded with four sizing handles that can be used to move and size the placeholder.	True	False
6.	A tab stop is a stopping point along a line to which text will indent when you press ⏎Enter.	True	False
7.	Running a slide show makes the slide fill the screen, hiding the PowerPoint application window, so you can view the slides as your audience would.	True	False
8.	The size of a placeholder can be changed by dragging its sizing handles.	True	False
9.	The font is the height of the character and is commonly measured in points.	True	False
10.	A drawing object is an illustration such as a scanned photograph.	True	False

Discussion Questions

1. Suppose that you were required to present a report in your economics class and that you have decided to do an electronic presentation. Discuss each of the presentation development steps you would follow. Be as specific as possible.

2. List the different PowerPoint views. Define each and describe how they are typically used.

3. How can fonts and graphics be used to enhance a presentation?

Hands-On Practice Exercises

Step-by-Step

Rating System   ☆ Easy
☆☆ Moderate
☆☆☆ Difficult

☆

1. Jodie Lau is the administrative assistant for a doctor. She is giving a presentation on Alzheimer's disease to a support group. She has asked for your help to make the presentation more visually appealing. Several slides of the completed presentation are shown here.

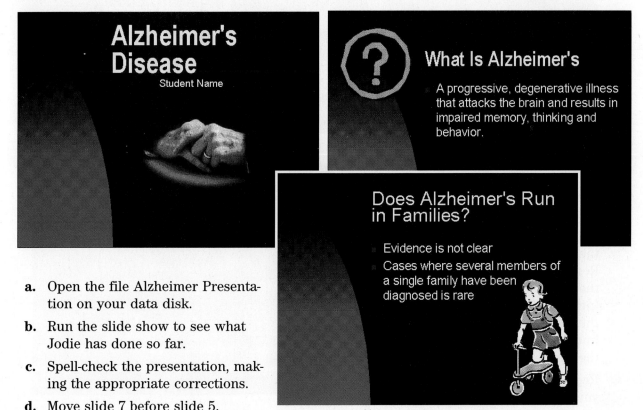

a. Open the file Alzheimer Presentation on your data disk.

b. Run the slide show to see what Jodie has done so far.

c. Spell-check the presentation, making the appropriate corrections.

d. Move slide 7 before slide 5.

e. Enter your name as the subtitle in slide 1. Insert the Hands.jpg picture from your data disk on the title slide. Size and position it appropriately.

f. Reduce the title font size of slides 6 and 7 to 44 pt. Size the placeholder to display the title on two lines.

  g. Insert the Question Marks clip art in the Symbols category on slide 3. Size and position it appropriately. Insert the Children clip art in the Home and Family category on slide 7. (Both ClipArt graphics are also available on your data disk.) Size and position it appropriately.

  h. Run the slide show.

  i. Save the presentation as Alzheimer Presentation1. Print the slides as handouts (four per page).

  j. You will complete this presentation in Practice Exercise 1 of Tutorial 2.

☆

2. You work for the career services center of a university and you are planning a presentation on how to write effective resumes and cover letters. A previous employee had started to create such a presentation, but never got around to editing or finalizing it. You need to clean it up and enhance it a bit before presenting it. Several slides of the completed presentation are shown here.

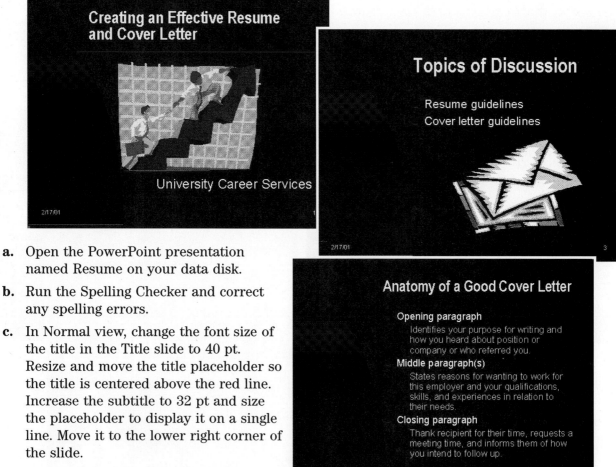

  a. Open the PowerPoint presentation named Resume on your data disk.

  b. Run the Spelling Checker and correct any spelling errors.

  c. In Normal view, change the font size of the title in the Title slide to 40 pt. Resize and move the title placeholder so the title is centered above the red line. Increase the subtitle to 32 pt and size the placeholder to display it on a single line. Move it to the lower right corner of the slide.

  d. Replace "Student Name" in slide 2 with your name.

  e. On slide 5, remove the bullet format from the three demoted bulleted paragraphs. Insert a tab at the beginning of each of these paragraphs so they are indented.

  f. Since there is too much text on slide 6, remove the demoted bulleted paragraphs under "Identifying Information," "Objectives," and "Experience" (you can elaborate on these during your presentation).

  g. Reorganize the bulleted items on slide 9 so that "Types of cover letters" is the first item. To match the slide order with the way the topics are now introduced, move slide 12 before slide 10.

h. In Normal view, remove the bullet format from the three demoted bulleted paragraphs on slide 10, and insert a tab at the beginning of each of these paragraphs so they are indented correctly. Remove the periods at the end of the paragraphs (because they are not complete sentences).

i. Remove the bullet format from the three demoted bulleted paragraphs on slide 12, and insert a tab at the beginning of each of these paragraphs so they are indented correctly. Remove the period at the end of the demoted items.

j. Change the font size of the "Anatomy of a Good Cover Letter" title to 36 pt so it all fits on one line. Resize the bullet placeholder box so all the text fits within it, and move it up so it does not end so close to the bottom.

k. On the title slide, insert the Working Towards Goals clip art from the Business category (or from your data disk). Resize and position it above the subtitle.

l. On slide 3, insert the Correspondence clip art in the Communications category (or from your data disk) below the bulleted list. Size and position it appropriately.

m. Save the presentation as Final Resume.

n. Run the slide show.

o. Print the slides as handouts (six per page) and close the presentation.

☆ ☆

3. As the manager of the Downtown Internet Cafe, you want to make a presentation to the other employees about the various blends of coffee that the cafe offers. The purpose of this presentation is to enable employees to answer the many questions that are asked by customers when looking at the Blend of the Day board or choosing the type of coffee beans they want to purchase. Several slides of the completed presentation are shown here.

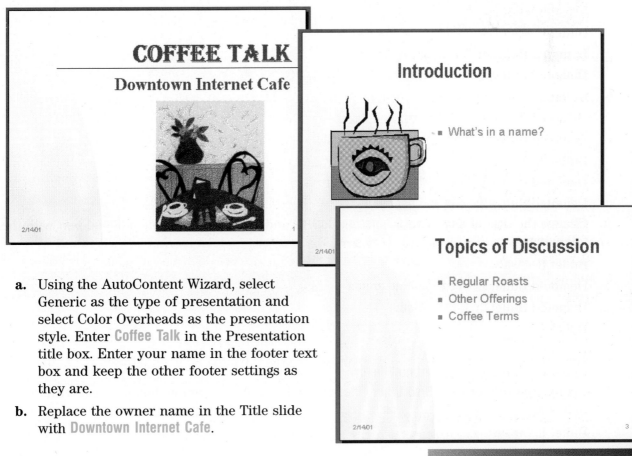

a. Using the AutoContent Wizard, select Generic as the type of presentation and select Color Overheads as the presentation style. Enter Coffee Talk in the Presentation title box. Enter your name in the footer text box and keep the other footer settings as they are.

b. Replace the owner name in the Title slide with Downtown Internet Cafe.

c. Replace the sample bulleted text on slide 2 with the following:

Bullet 1: What's in a name?

d. Replace the sample bulleted text on slide 3 with the following:

Bullet 1: Regular Roasts

Bullet 2: Other Offerings

e. Switch to Slide Sorter view. Change the title of slide 4 to Regular Roasts and replace the sample bulleted text with the following:

Bullet 1: Central and South American

Bullet 2: East African

Bullet 3: Indonesian

f. Change the title of slide 5 to Central and South American Coffees and replace the sample bulleted text with the following:

Bullet 1: Colombian

Demoted Bullet 1: Distinctive, heady aroma

Demoted Bullet 2 Clean, mellow, balanced flavor

Bullet 2: Guatemala Antigua

Demoted Bullet 1: Rich and satisfying

Demoted Bullet 2: Lively flavor

Bullet 3: Kona

Demoted Bullet 1: Delicately aromatic

Demoted Bullet 2: Smooth, mild flavor

g. Change the title of slide 6 to East African Coffees and replace the sample bulleted text with the following:

Bullet 1: Arabian

Demoted Bullet 1: Strong and sparkling

Demoted Bullet 2: Pungent, winy flavor

Bullet 2: Ethiopian

Demoted Bullet 1: Floral aroma and flavor

Demoted Bullet 2: Moderate body and acidity

Bullet 3: Kenyan

Demoted Bullet 1: Intense flavor and acidity

Demoted Bullet 2: Rich and hearty

h. Change the title of slide 7 to Indonesian Coffees and replace the sample bulleted text with the following:

Bullet 1: Java

Demoted Bullet 1: Deep, fragrant aroma

Demoted Bullet 2: Rich-bodied

Bullet 2: Sumatra

Demoted Bullet 1: Herbal aroma

Demoted Bullet 2: Spicy, vibrant flavor

i. Change the title of slide 8 to Other Offerings and replace the sample bulleted text with the following:

Bullet 1: Blends

Bullet 2: Dark Roasts

Demoted Bullet 1: Espresso (dark)

Demoted Bullet 2: Italian (darker)

Demoted Bullet 3: French (darkest)

Bullet 3: Decaffeinated

Demoted Bullet 1: Traditionally (solvent) processed

Demoted Bullet 2: Water processed

Demoted Bullet 3: Regular and dark roasts

j. Change the order of the last two demoted bulleted items in slide 6.

k. Add a second bullet to slide 2 with the following text:

Bullet 2: Coffee Terms

l. Change the title of slide 9 to Coffee Terms and replace the sample bulleted text with the following:

Bullet 1: Flavor

    A coffee's aroma, acidity, and body

Bullet 2: Aroma

    The odor or fragrance of brewed coffee

Bullet 3: Acidity

    The sharp, lively characteristic of coffee

Bullet 4: Body

    The impression of a coffee's weight in the mouth

m. Change the font size of the bulleted terms in slide 9 to 24 pt and the indented definitions to 20 pt.

n. Change the font and size of the title and subtitle on the title slide to improve its appearance.

o. On the title slide, insert the clip art Coffee Shop from your data disk. Resize and position it below the subtitle.

p. Insert the clip art Coffee Mug from your data disk. Appropriately size and position the bulleted items and clip art on the slide.

q. Insert the clip art Cup from your data disk. Appropriately size and position the clip art on the slide.

r. Run the Spelling Checker and correct any spelling errors.

s. Save the presentation as Coffee.

t. Run the slide show.

u. Print the slides as handouts (six per page).

You will complete this presentation in Practice Exercise 3 of Tutorial 2.

☆ ☆ ☆

4. Carol Hayes is the program coordinator for Fitness Lifestyles, a physical conditioning and health center. She has noticed that clients are not coming in as regularly as they used to. To try and curb this trend, Carol has decided to give a presentation to the fitness trainers about the importance of maintaining an exercise program so they can pass this on to clients. Several slides of the completed presentation are shown here.

a. Using the AutoContent Wizard, select Product and Services Overview as the type of presentation, and select On-screen as the presentation style. Enter Why Exercise? in the Presentation title box. Add your name as the footer text and keep the other footer selections as they are.

b. In Normal view, replace the owner name in the Title slide with Presented by Lifestyle Fitness. On slide 2, replace the title with What Ongoing Exercise Can Do for You and the sample bulleted list with the following:

Bullet 1: Benefits

Bullet 2: Programs

c. Replace the title of slide 3 with Benefits and the sample bulleted text with the following:

Bullet 1: Prevents heart disease and normalizes blood pressure

Bullet 2: Regulates blood sugar and controls body weight

Bullet 3: Prevents bone and muscle tissue loss

Bullet 4: Slows aging and improves lifestyle

d. Replace the title of slide 4 with Prevent Heart Disease and Normalize Blood Pressure and the sample bulleted text with the following:

Bullet 1: Slows plaque buildup in arteries

Bullet 2: Increases "good" and decreases "bad" cholesterol

Bullet 3: Decreases resting heart rate

Bullet 4: Prevents obstructive blood clots

Bullet 5: Makes heart stronger and more efficient

e. Insert two new slides as slides 5 and 6 using the Bulleted List layout.

f. Enter the title of slide 5 as Regulate Blood Sugar and Control Body Weight and the following three bulleted items:

Bullet 1: Improves body's ability to metabolize sugar

Bullet 2: Burns calories

Bullet 3: Maintains weight loss

g. Enter the title of slide 6 as Prevent Bone and Muscle Tissue Loss and the following three bulleted items:

Bullet 1: Prevents drop in metabolic rate

Bullet 2: Prevents loss of lean body mass

Bullet 3: Prevents osteoporosis

h. Change the title of slide 7 to Slow Aging and the sample bulleted text to the following:

Bullet 1: Increases stamina, strength, flexibility, bone density, and metabolic rate

Bullet 2: Helps you stay active

Bullet 3: Promotes enthusiasm for living

i. Change the title of slide 8 to Improve Lifestyle and the sample bulleted text to the following:

Bullet 1: Makes activity easier

Bullet 2: Increases stress resistance

Bullet 3: Improves sleep

Bullet 4: Encourages other healthy habits

j. Change the title of slide 9 to Programs and the bulleted text to the following:

Bullet 1: Personalized fitness programs

Bullet 2: Group workout classes

Bullet 3: Running and racquetball clubs

k. In Slide Sorter view, delete the "Slow Aging" slide (7).

l. In Normal view, delete "Slows Aging and" from the Benefits slide (3). Capitalize the letter I in "improves."

m. In Slide Sorter view, insert a slide after slide 8 using the Bulleted List layout. In Normal view, change the title of slide 8 to Exercise Makes Life More Fun! Size the title placeholder so the title appears on one line. Replace the sample bulleted text with the following:

Bullet 1: Start a regular workout program today

Bullet 2: Join a workout group and share the health

Insert the clip art Hikers from your data disk. Resize and position it to the right of the bullets.

n. Increase the title on the title slide to 60 pt. Increase the subtitle to 40 pt and change the font to Times New Roman. Insert the clip art Runners from your data disk. Appropriately size and position the subtitle and clip art on the slide.

o. On slide 2, insert the clip art Opportunity from the Metaphor category. Size it appropriately.

p. Insert the clip art Blood Pressure from your data disk on slide 3. Appropriately size and position the bulleted items and clip art on the slide.

q. Change the order of the bulleted items on slide 6 so the first item is "Prevents Osteoporosis."

r. Switch the order of slides 4 and 5.

s. Run the Spelling Checker and correct any spelling errors.

t. Save the presentation as Exercise.

u. Run the slide show.

v. Print the slides as handouts (three per page).

You will complete this presentation in Practice Exercise 4 of Tutorial 2.

☆ ☆ ☆

5. Damon Limbi is the marketing manager of The Sports Company, a large sporting goods store. He has asked you to make a presentation at the weekly sales meeting about the sales competition. Several slides of the completed presentation are shown here. To begin the presentation, complete the steps below.

a. Using the AutoContent Wizard, select Generic as the type of presentation, and select Color Overheads as the type of output for the presentation. Enter Market Analysis in the Presentation Title text box. Enter your name in the footer text box. Keep the other footer options as they are.

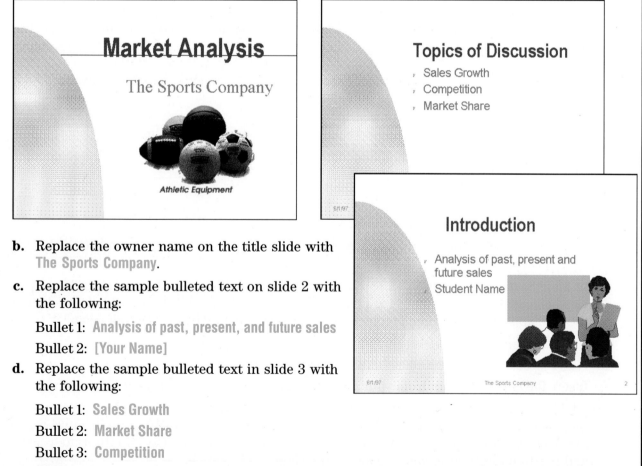

b. Replace the owner name on the title slide with The Sports Company.

c. Replace the sample bulleted text on slide 2 with the following:

Bullet 1: Analysis of past, present, and future sales

Bullet 2: [Your Name]

d. Replace the sample bulleted text in slide 3 with the following:

Bullet 1: Sales Growth

Bullet 2: Market Share

Bullet 3: Competition

e. Change the order of the bullets on slide 3 so that "Competition" is above "Market Share."

f. Switch to Slide view. Change the title of slide 4 to Sales Growth. Turn off the bullets and display the ruler if necessary. Create a left tab at the 1-inch mark and a right tab at the 5-inch mark. Enter the following (remember to press Tab before each line and after the word "sales"):

1997 sales	$5,100,000
1998 sales	$5,900,000
1999 sales	$7,400,000
2000 sales	$10,200,000

g. Change the title of slide 5 to Competition and replace the sample bulleted text with the following:

Bullet 1: Action Corporation

Demoted Bullet 1: Established in 1986

Demoted Bullet 2: Located in Union, Oregon

Bullet 2: Team Unlimited

Demoted Bullet 1: Established in 1989

Demoted Bullet 2: Located in Spring, Maine

h. Change the title of slide 6 to Market Share and replace the sample bulleted text with the following:

Bullet 1: 35% Sports Company

Bullet 2: 30% Action Corporation

Bullet 3: 25% Teams Unlimited

Bullet 4: 10% Other

i. In Slide Sorter view, delete slide 7 and move the new slide 7 to after slide 8.

j. Switch to Normal view. Replace the sample bulleted text on slide 7 with the following:

Bullet 1: Research Industry Trends

Bullet 2: Detail Strengths and Weaknesses

Bullet 3: Develop Future Marketing Plan

k. Replace the sample bulleted text on slide 8 with the following:

Bullet 1: Past—sales doubled in 4 years

Bullet 2: Present—market share 35%

Bullet 3: Future—where to go from here?

l. Change the font of the subtitle on the title slide to Times New Roman and the size to 44. Size the placeholder to display the subtitle on one line.

m. Insert the Equipment clip art from your data disk below the subtitle. Size it appropriately.

n. Add the Presentations clip art from your data disk appropriately on slide 2 and size it.

o. Run the slide show.

p. Save the presentation as Marketing Presentation.

q. Print the slides as handouts (four per page).

You will complete this presentation in Practice Exercise 5 of Tutorial 2.

On Your Own

☆

6. As owner of the Better Bikes Company, you have written several articles for your local newspaper on bicycle safety. Based on one of your articles, an elementary school in your town has asked you to do a presentation for their PTA meeting on children's cycling tips. Create your presentation in PowerPoint, using the following article excerpt as a resource. Use the AutoContent Wizard and the Generic template. Include your name in the footer. When you are done, run the Spelling Checker, then save and print your presentation.

It is important to reinforce, expand, and continue your children's natural love for bicycling and make your outings more enjoyable. Here are some suggestions:

- Introduce your infants to bicycling by carrying them in a bicycle seat or trailer, and continue to ride with your children as they grow.
- When your children are ready for their own bikes, make sure they are the proper size.
- Emphasize the fun of riding rather than technique or mileage.
- Combine bicycling with other activities, such as going on a picnic or riding to the zoo or park.

To teach your children proper safety and steadiness skills, you can play the "bike lane game." Draw an imaginary lane with sidewalk chalk on a flat, smooth surface and have your children:

- Ride in a straight line without wobbling.
- Stop and start on command in a controlled manner.
- Look over their left shoulders to "read" how many fingers you're holding up behind them (which helps them develop the technique of looking back at traffic).
- Practice proper hand signals.
- Ride around and between objects (such as sponges) randomly placed in the course (which helps them learn to negotiate objects).

Some cycling tips geared toward keeping your children safe on the streets are:

- Encourage your children to wear a helmet by letting them select their own, letting them put decals on the outer shell, pointing out cyclists who are wearing helmets, and always wearing your own helmet when riding your bicycle.
- Equip your children's bicycles with bells or a horn, a safety flag, reflective spoke beads, and a good lock.
- Teach your children basic bicycle safety tips (such as riding with the traffic, riding on the shoulder if it's wide and clean, never riding on a sidewalk, and keeping both hands on the handlebars unless you are signaling for a turn or stop). Keep a copy of the BASIC BIKING SAFETY brochure handy and review it with your children periodically. For a copy of this brochure, contact Better Bikes at (602) 555-7272.

You will complete this presentation in Practice Exercise 7 of Tutorial 2.

☆ ☆

7. You are a trainer with Super Software, Inc. You received a memo from your manager alerting you that many of the support personnel are not using proper telephone protocol or obtaining the proper information from the customers who call in. Your manager has asked you to conduct a training class that covers these topics. Using the Memo data file as a resource, prepare the slides for your class. Use the AutoContent Wizard and select an appropriate presentation type. Include your name in the footer. When you are done, save the presentation and print the handouts.

 ☆ ☆

8. You are a counselor at Financial Consultants and you have been asked to prepare a presentation on family financial planning. Contact a financial planning company or research this topic on the Web and find out basic budget guidelines for a middle-income family. Use the AutoContent Wizard to create an onscreen presentation from the information you gathered. Use the Recommending a Strategy presentation type and include your name in the footer. Edit the slides to include the content for your presentation. Add appropriate clip art. Save your presentation and print the handouts. (You will expand it in Practice Exercise 8 in Tutorial 2.)

 ☆ ☆ ☆

9. You work at a job placement agency, and you have been asked to do a presentation for new clients that describes the services your company offers and the categories used to list available jobs. Visit a local placement agency or search the Web to gather information about job placement agency services and job listings. Using the AutoContent Wizard, select an appropriate presentation type to create a short presentation. Include your name in the footer. When you are done, save the presentation and print the handouts.

 ☆ ☆ ☆

10. Your company wants to create a Web site, but it is not sure whether to design its own or hire a Web design firm to do it. You have been asked to create a presentation to management relaying the pros and cons of each approach. To gather information, search the Web for the topic "Web design" and select some key points about designing a Web page from one of the "how-to" or "tips" categories. Use these points to create the first part of your presentation and call it something like "Creating Our Own Web Page." Then search the Web for the topic "Web designers" and select two Web design firms. Pick some key points about each firm (for example, Web sites they have designed, design elements they typically use, and/or their design philosophy). Finally, include at least one slide that lists the pros and cons of each approach. Include your name on the title slide. When your presentation is complete, save and print the slide as handouts. (You will expand on it in Practice Exercise 9 of Tutorial 2.)

Modifying and Refining a Presentation

Competencies

After completing this tutorial, you will know how to:

1. Find and replace text.
2. Change the slide layout.
3. Create and enhance a table.
4. Modify clip art and create a text box.
5. Change the presentation's design and color scheme.
6. Change slide and title masters.
7. Hide the title slide footer.
8. Duplicate and hide slides.
9. Create and enhance drawing objects.
10. Add animation and sound.
11. Add transitions and builds.
12. Control and annotate a slide show.
13. Create speaker notes.
14. Check the style.
15. Document the file and print selected slides.

Case Study

The agency director was very impressed with your first draft of the presentation to recruit volunteers, and asked to see the presentation onscreen. While viewing it the director made several suggestions to improve both content and design. First, the director wants you to include more information on ways

Tables in presentations make data easy to understand.

Slide designs and color schemes enhance the look of a presentation.

Slide transitions, builds, and special effects add action to a slide show.

that volunteers can help. Additionally, because the agency has such an excellent adoption rate, the director suggests that you include a table to illustrate the success of the adoption program. It was also suggested that you consider using a different design background and that you include more art and other graphic features to enhance the appearance of the slides. Finally, to keep the audience's attention, the director suggests that you look at adding more action to the slides using the special effects included with PowerPoint.

PowerPoint 2000 gives you the design and production capabilities to create a first-class onscreen presentation. These features include artist-designed layouts and color schemes that give your presentation a professional appearance. In addition, you can add your own personal touches by modifying text attributes, incorporating art or graphics, and including animation to add impact, interest, and excitement to your presentation.

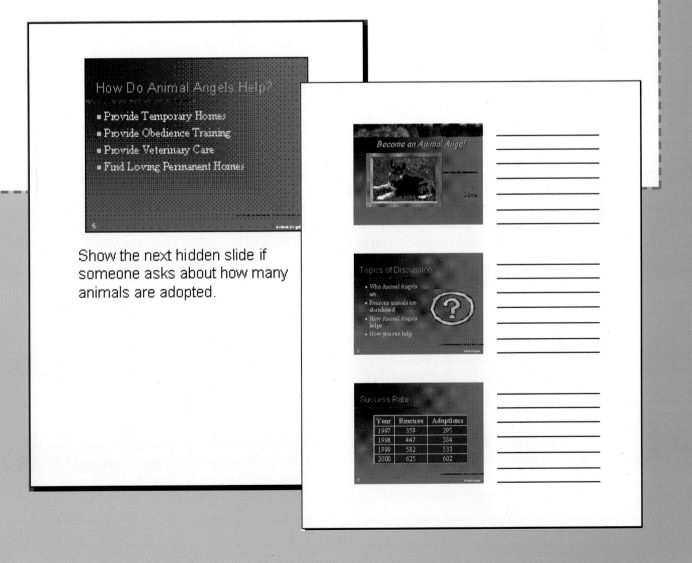

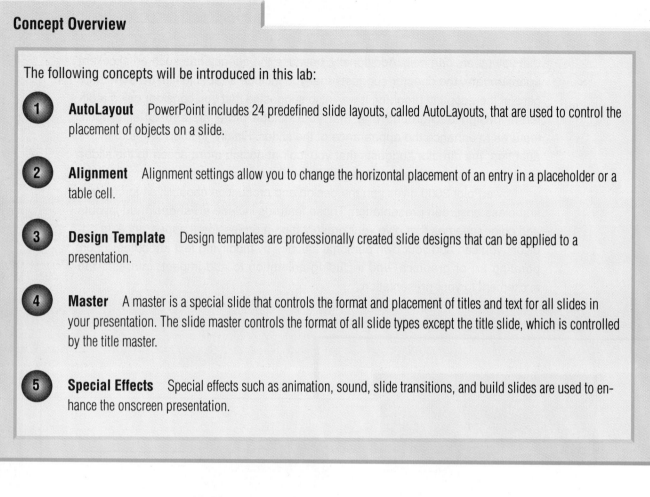

Concept Overview

The following concepts will be introduced in this lab:

1   **AutoLayout**   PowerPoint includes 24 predefined slide layouts, called AutoLayouts, that are used to control the placement of objects on a slide.

2   **Alignment**   Alignment settings allow you to change the horizontal placement of an entry in a placeholder or a table cell.

3   **Design Template**   Design templates are professionally created slide designs that can be applied to a presentation.

4   **Master**   A master is a special slide that controls the format and placement of titles and text for all slides in your presentation. The slide master controls the format of all slide types except the title slide, which is controlled by the title master.

5   **Special Effects**   Special effects such as animation, sound, slide transitions, and build slides are used to enhance the onscreen presentation.

Using Find and Replace

You have updated the content to include the additional information on ways that volunteers can help Animal Angels. To see the revised presentation,

1   Load PowerPoint 2000.

   Put your data disk in drive A (or the appropriate drive for your system).

   Open the file Volunteer2 from your data disk.

   If necessary, switch to Normal view.

   Replace Student Name in the outline pane of slide 1 with your name.

As you look at the text in the slides, you decide to edit the presentation by replacing the word "pet" in many locations with the word "animal." To do this quickly, you will use the Find and Replace feature to find the text you specify and automatically replace it with other text.

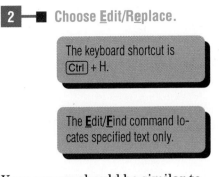

2 Choose <u>E</u>dit/R<u>e</u>place.

The keyboard shortcut is
Ctrl + H.

The <u>E</u>dit/<u>F</u>ind command lo-
cates specified text only.

Your screen should be similar to
Figure 2–1.

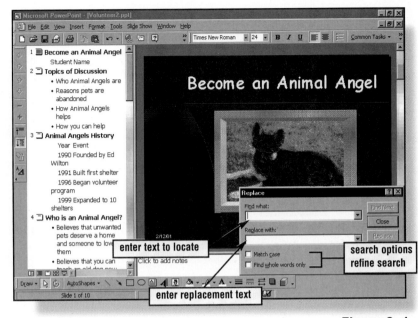

enter text to locate

enter replacement text

search options
refine search

Figure 2–1

In the Find What text box, you enter the text you want to locate. The two
options described in the table below allow you to refine how the search
for the text you want to locate is conducted.

Option	Effect on Text
Match Case	Distinguishes between uppercase and lowercase characters. When selected, finds only those instances in which the capitalization matches the text you typed in the Find What box.
Find Whole Words Only	Distinguishes between whole and partial words. When selected, locates matches that are whole words and not part of a larger word. For example, finds "cat" only and not "catastrophe" too.

The text you want to replace is entered in the Replace With text box. The
replacement text must be entered exactly as you want it to appear in your
document. You want to find all occurrences of the complete word "pet"
and replace them with the word "animal." To enter the text to find and replace and begin the search,

3 ■ Type **pet** in the Find What text box.

> After entering the text to find, do not press ⏎Enter or this will choose Find Next and the search will begin.

■ Type **animal** in the Replace With text box.

■ Click Find Next Find Next.

■ If necessary, move the dialog box so you can see the located text.

Your screen should be similar to Figure 2–2.

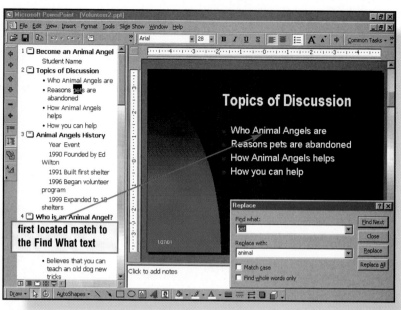

Figure 2–2

> Find and Replace will highlight located text in whichever pane is current when the procedure is started.

Immediately, the first occurrence of text in the presentation that matches the entry in the Find What text box is located and highlighted in the outline pane. To replace the located word with the replacement text,

4 ■ Click Replace.

Your screen should be similar to Figure 2–3.

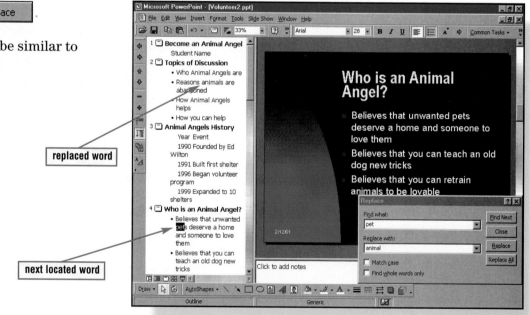

Figure 2–3

The highlighted text is replaced, and the next occurrence of the Find text is located in slide 4. However, you do not want to replace this occurrence.

5 ■ Click [Find Next] to continue.

■ Replace the third located word in slide 6.

■ Skip the fourth located word in slide 7.

■ Replace the last located word in slide 8.

The program begins searching at the beginning again and is highlighting the word "pet" in slide 4 that you originally skipped. To end the process,

6 ■ Click [Close].

If you are changing all the occurrences, it is much faster to use the Replace All command button. Exercise care when using Replace All, because the search text you specify might be part of another word and you may accidentally replace text you want to keep.

Selecting a Slide Layout

During your discussion with the agency director, it was suggested that you add a slide containing data on the number of adoptions versus rescues. To include this information in the presentation, you will insert a new slide after slide 5.

1 ■ Display slide 5.

■ Click ![icon] New Slide.

> You can also choose New Slide from the Common Tasks drop-down list button.

Your screen should be similar to Figure 2–4.

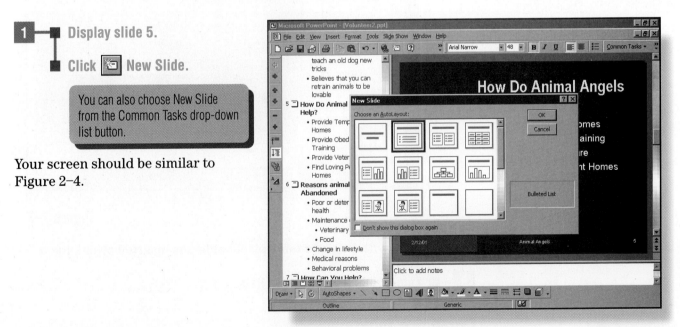

Figure 2–4

The slide AutoLayout options are displayed in the New Slide dialog box. The default slide layout, Bulleted List, is selected.

Concept ① AutoLayout

PowerPoint includes 24 predefined slide layouts called **AutoLayouts** that are used to control the placement of objects on a slide. For example, there is a layout that includes placeholders for a title and bulleted text, and another with placeholders for a title, text, and clip art.

You can change the layout of an existing slide. If the new layout does not include placeholders for objects that are already on your slide (for example, if you created a chart and then realize that the new layout does not include a chart placeholder), you do not lose the information. All objects remain on the slide, and you can rearrange them to fit the new layout.

To make creating slides easy, use the predefined layouts. The layouts help you keep your presentation format consistent and, therefore, more professional.

Because this slide will contain a table showing the adoption figures, you want to use the table slide layout.

 **Double-click** 🔲 **Table.**

Your screen should be similar to Figure 2–5.

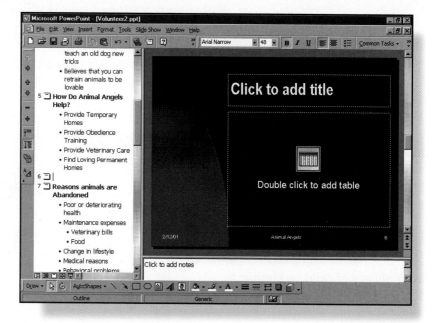

Figure 2–5

A new slide 6 with title and table placeholders is inserted after slide 5.

 Enter the title text **Success Rate.**

Creating a Table

Next you want to create a table to display the number of adoptions and rescues. A table is made up of rows and columns of cells that you can fill with text and graphics. Traditionally, columns are identified from left to right beginning with the letter A, and rows are numbered from top to bottom beginning with the number 1. Tables are commonly used to align numbers in columns and then sort and perform calculations on them. They make it easier to read and understand numbers.

1 ■— Double-click the table placeholder.

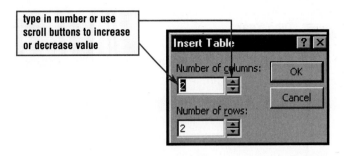

type in number or use scroll buttons to increase or decrease value

In the Insert Table dialog box you specify the number of rows and columns for the table.

2 ■— Specify 3 columns and 5 rows.

■ Click [OK].

■ If necessary, move the Tables and Borders toolbar out of the way or dock it.

Your screen should be similar to Figure 2–6.

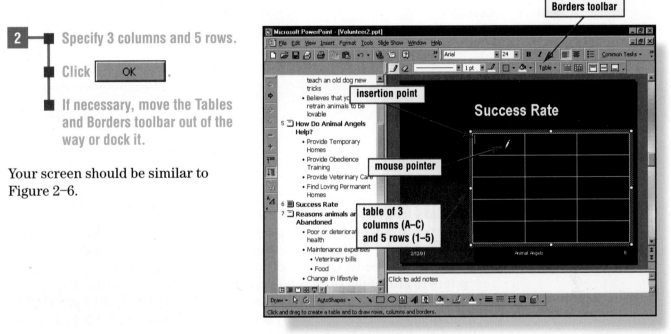

Figure 2–6

If the Tables and Borders toolbar is not displayed automatically, you will need to open it from the Toolbar shortcut menu.

A blank table consisting of three columns and five rows is displayed as a selected object. The Tables and Borders toolbar is displayed. The mouse pointer appears as a Draw table tool ⁄ so you can add more rows and columns by dragging to specify the location you want.

To move in a table, click on the cell or use [Tab ↹] to move to the next cell to the right and [⇧Shift] + [Tab ↹] to move to the preceding cell. You can also use the [↑] and [↓] directional keys to move up or down a row. The insertion point appears in the top left corner cell ready for you to enter text. You can now enter the information into the table.

3 ▪ Type **Year**

▪ Press (Tab ⇥) or click on the next cell to the right.

> Pressing (Enter) adds a new line to the current cell.

▪ Add the rest of the information shown below to the table.

	Column A	Column B	Column C
		Rescues	**Adoptions**
row 2	**1997**	**359**	**295**
row 3	**1998**	**447**	**384**
row 4	**1999**	**582**	**533**
row 5	**2000**	**625**	**602**

Your screen should be similar to Figure 2–7.

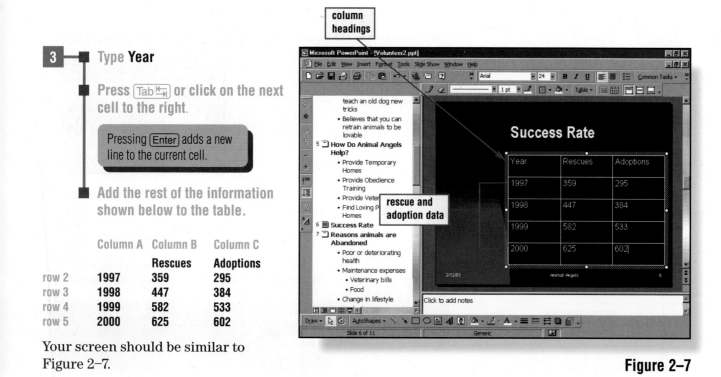

Figure 2–7

Enhancing a Table

Next you want to improve the table's appearance by modifying the attributes associated with the table text. An **attribute** is a feature associated with text or an object that can be enhanced using menu commands and drawing tools. Fonts and font size are two basic text attributes that you have used already. Other text attributes are text color and style. **Style** refers to attributes such as bold and italics. You can also apply special effects such as shadows and embossed text effects to text. The Format/Font command is used to add many of these text effects. In addition, there are toolbar shortcuts for the most frequently used features.

1

Drag to select row 1 containing the column headings and increase the font size to 36 pt.

Click **B** Bold to bold the selection.

> The menu equivalent is F**o**rmat/**F**ont/F**o**nt Style/Bold and the keyboard shortcut is [Ctrl] + B.

Click **A** ▼ Font Color (in the Drawing toolbar).

Change the font color of the table headings to pale yellow to match the slide title.

> The menu equivalent is F**o**rmat/**F**ont/**C**olor.

Select rows 2 through 5 and increase the font size to 32.

Clear the selection.

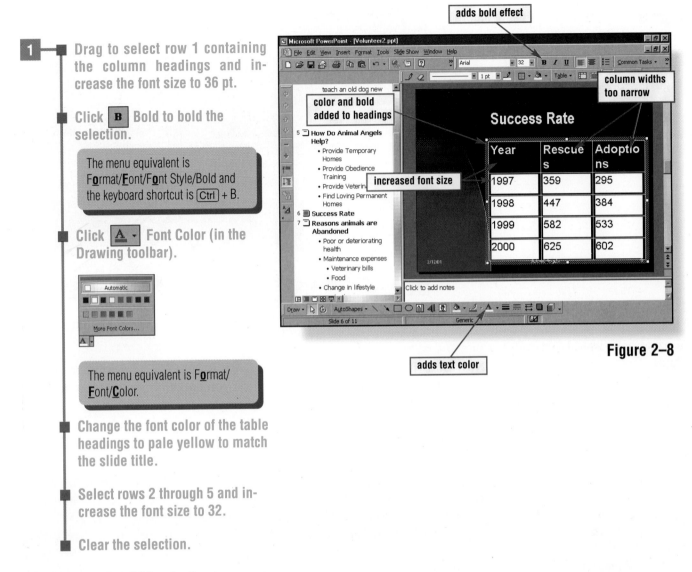

Figure 2–8

Your screen should be similar to Figure 2–8.

Because you increased the font size of the headings, two of the headings are too large to display on a single line in the cell space. To fix this, you will adjust the size of the columns to fit their contents. To adjust the column width or row height, drag the row and column boundaries. The mouse pointer appears as a ◂‖▸ when you can size the column and ⇰ when you can size the row.

2 Size the columns using Figure 2–9 as a guide.

Your screen should be similar to Figure 2–9.

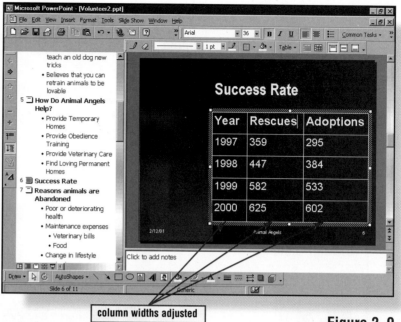

column widths adjusted

Figure 2–9

Now that the columns are more appropriately sized, you want to center the text and data in the cells. To do this you can change the alignment of the entries.

Concept ② Alignment

Alignment settings allow you to change the horizontal placement of an entry in a placeholder or a table cell. There are four different alignment settings: left, center, right, and justified.

Alignment		Effect on Text
Left		Aligns text against the left edge of the placeholder or cell, leaving the right edge of text that wraps to another line ragged.
Center		Centers each line of text between the left and right edge of the placeholder or cell.
Right		Aligns text against the right edge of the placeholder or cell, leaving the left edge of multiple lines ragged.
Justified		Aligns text evenly with both the right and left edge of the placeholder or cell.

The commands to change alignment settings are options under the Format/Alignment menu. However, it is much faster to use the shortcuts shown below.

Alignment	Keyboard Shortcut	Button
Left	Ctrl + L	
Center	Ctrl + E	
Right	Ctrl + R	
Justified	Ctrl + J	

3 Select the entire table contents.

Click Center.

Your screen should be similar to Figure 2–10.

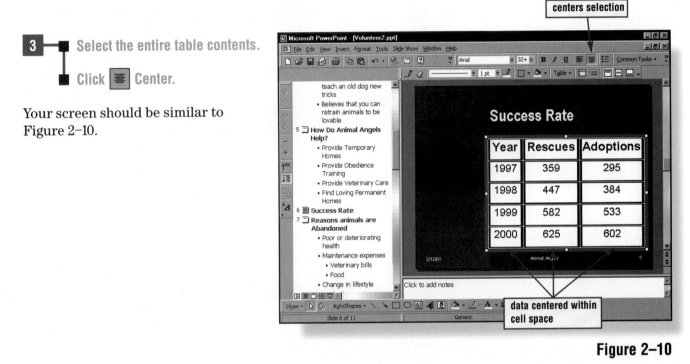

Figure 2–10

Finally, you will add a background color to the table and a color to the outside border. You will also increase the thickness or weight of the borderline. The Tables and Borders toolbar is used to make these enhancements.

4

Click [1 pt ▾] Border Width and select 3 pt to increase the weight of the border.

Click [🖉] Border Color and select orange.

> You can also use the **T**able command on the **F**ormat menu to add fills and borders.

Point to the outside top border and drag along the border to apply the new settings over the existing border.

> The mouse pointer is a 🖉 when you can draw over the border. A dotted line identifies the section of the border that will be modified.

In the same manner, apply the new border formats to the remaining three sides of the table.

Click [🖉] Draw Table to turn off the Draw Table feature.

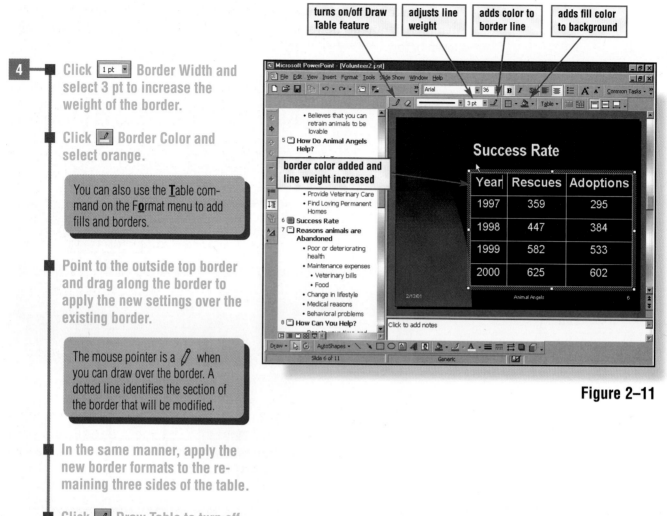

Figure 2–11

Your screen should be similar to Figure 2–11.

Next you will add a background fill color to the table.

5 Select the entire table.

Click Fill Color and select a darker blue color.

Adjust the position of the table on the slide as in Figure 2–12.

Clear the selection.

Your screen should be similar to Figure 2–12.

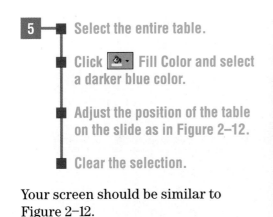

Figure 2–12

The enhancements you added to the table greatly improve its appearance.

Changing Slide Layout

You would also like to add a clip art drawing to slide 2. Before doing this you will change the slide layout from the bulleted list style to a style that is designed to accommodate both text and clip art.

1 Display slide 2.

Click Common Tasks and choose Slide Layout.

> The menu equivalent is Format/Slide Layout.

Select Text & Clip Art (first layout in third row).

Click Apply.

Your screen should be similar to Figure 2–13.

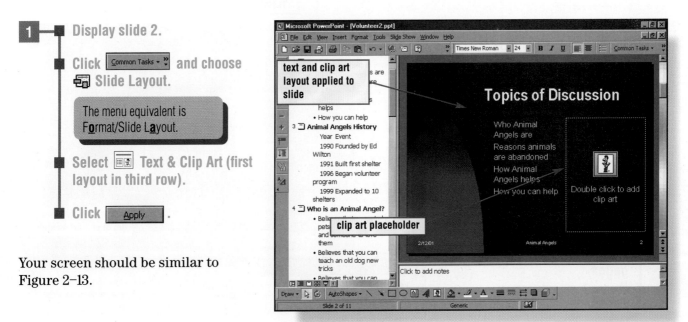

Figure 2–13

All the text has moved into the bullet placeholder on the left side of the slide, and the text was resized to fit. A clip art placeholder has been inserted on the right. You are ready to add a new clip art image.

2 Double-click the clip art placeholder.

From the Categories list box, select Signs.

Select the Question Mark clip art.

Click [⬚] Insert Clip.

Your screen should be similar to Figure 2–14.

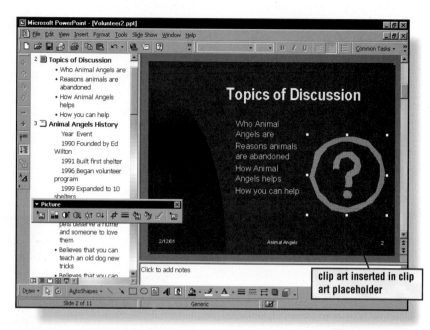

Figure 2–14

By changing the slide layout before inserting the clip art, you do not need to adjust the size of the clip art and the graphic does not overlap any text on the slide.

Modifying Clip Art

Now you want to change the color of the clip art graphic to a brighter color.

1 If necessary, display the Picture toolbar.

Click [⬚] Recolor Picture.

> The menu equivalent is Format/Picture/Recolor.

Open the shadow color drop-down menu and select a dark blue color.

Open the fill color drop-down menu and select the More Colors option.

Select a gold color from the Standard tab.

Click [OK].

Your screen should be similar to Figure 2–15.

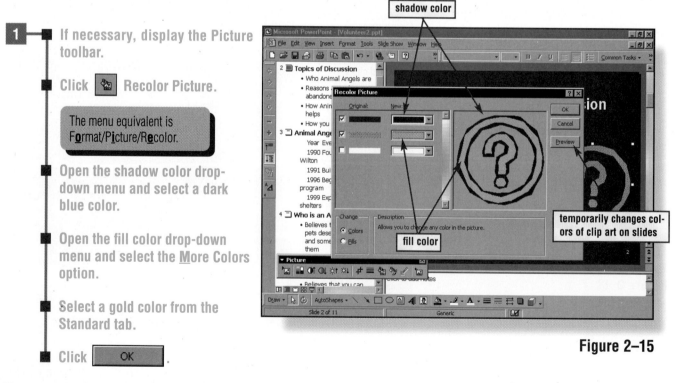

Figure 2–15

The preview area changes to match your selection. To see how the new colors look on the slide,

2 Click Preview .

Move the Recolor Picture dialog box out of the way to see the graphic on the slide.

Click OK .

Deselect the clip art and if necessary, turn off the Picture toolbar.

Finally, you want to reduce the size of the clip art and increase the size of the text placeholder. Using Figure 2–16 as a reference,

3 Reduce the size of the clip art placeholder.

Increase the size of the text placeholder.

Your screen should be similar to Figure 2–16.

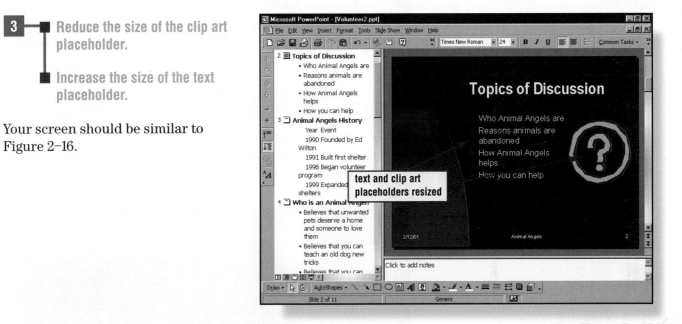

Figure 2–16

Creating a Text Box

On slide 11, you want to add the organization's name and address. To make it stand out on the slide, you will put it into a text box using the Text Box tool on the Drawing toolbar.

1 ■ Display slide 11.

■ Click in the slide pane.

■ Click 🖺 Text Box.

> The menu equivalent is Insert/text box.

■ Position the mouse pointer in a blank area below the bullets and drag to create a box.

Your screen should be similar to Figure 2–17.

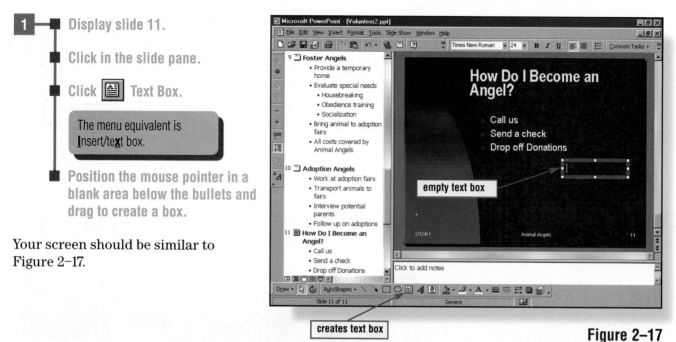

Figure 2–17

The text box is a selected object and is surrounded with a hatched border, indicating you can enter, delete, select, and format the text inside the box. It also displays an insertion point, indicating it is waiting for you to enter the text. As you type the text in the text box, it will automatically resize as needed to display the entire entry.

2 ■ Type the organization's name and address shown below in the text box. (Press ⏎Enter at the end of a line.)

Animal Angels
1166 Oak Street
Smitherton, NH 03112
(603) 555-1313

Your screen should be similar to Figure 2–18.

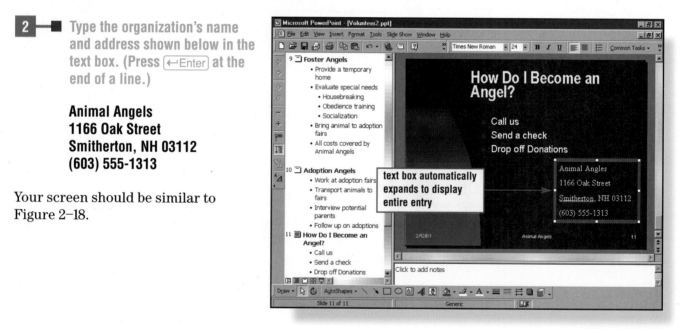

Figure 2–18

The text box expanded in size as you added text. Like any other object, it can be sized and moved anywhere on the slide. Notice that text that is attached to an object, such as a text box, is not displayed in the outline pane. You want to add a border around the box to define the space and add a fill color behind the text.

3  Click ▤ Line Style and select a style of your choice from the menu.

■ Click 🖎▾ Fill Color and select a color of your choice from the color palette.

■ If necessary, position the text box appropriately.

■ Click outside the text box.

Your screen should be similar to Figure 2–19.

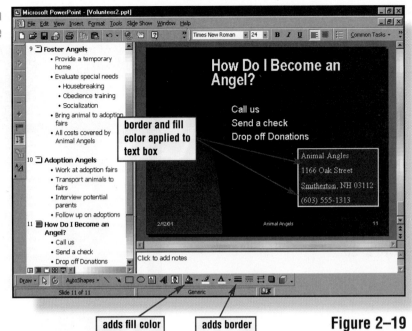

adds fill color   adds border   **Figure 2–19**

Changing the Presentation Design

Now you are satisfied with the presentation's basic content and organization. Next you want to change its style and appearance by applying a different design template.

Concept ③ Design Template

A **design template** is a professionally created slide design that can be applied to your presentation. Design templates contain color schemes, custom formatting, background designs, styled fonts, and other layout and design elements that have been created by artists. PowerPoint 2000 has more than 100 design templates from which you can select to quickly give your presentations a professional appearance. Selecting a design template changes all slides in your presentation to match the selected template design. This ensures that your presentation has a consistent look throughout.

To change the design template,

1 Move to slide 1.

Click [Common Tasks ▾]

Choose **Apply Design Template**.

> The menu equivalent is Format/Apply Design Template.

Your screen should be similar to Figure 2–20.

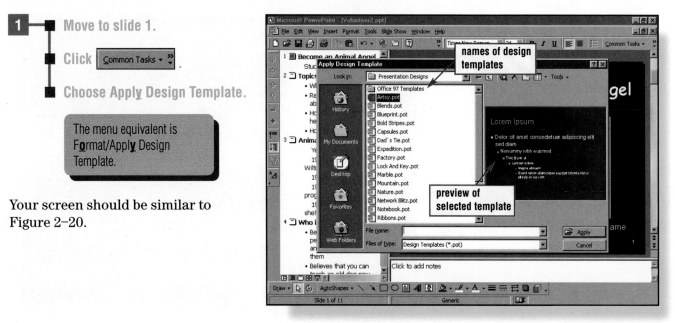

Figure 2–20

The Apply Design Template dialog box is similar to the File Open dialog box. In the list box are the names of the design templates located in the Presentation Designs folder. When a design template file name is selected, the preview box displays a sample of the colors, fonts, and designs for the selected design. The first design template in the list, Artsy, is the selected and displayed design template.

> The file extension for PowerPoint design templates is .pot.

2 Select several design templates to view in the preview box.

> Click on the design file name to select it.

After previewing the templates, you decide to use the Artsy template for your presentation. To use this template,

3 ━■ Double-click Artsy.pot.

Your screen should be similar to Figure 2–21.

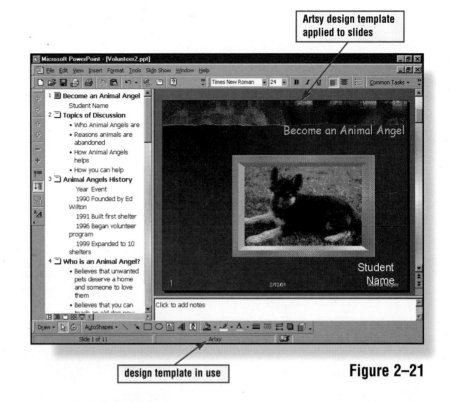

Artsy design template applied to slides

design template in use

Figure 2–21

The Artsy design template has been applied to all slides in the presentation. The status bar displays the name of the current design. When a new template design is applied, the text styles, graphics, and colors that are included in the template replace the previous template settings.

The picture on the title slide now covers part of the new design, and your name is covering some of the footer text. In addition, although the title is still the font you selected, its font size has been reduced and it is now too small. You will fix that shortly.

4 ━■ Move the picture and frame to the left side of the slide and your name up to just below the horizontal rule as shown in Figure 2–22.

> You can select multiple objects by holding down
> ⇧ Shift as you click on the objects.

Your screen should be similar to Figure 2–22.

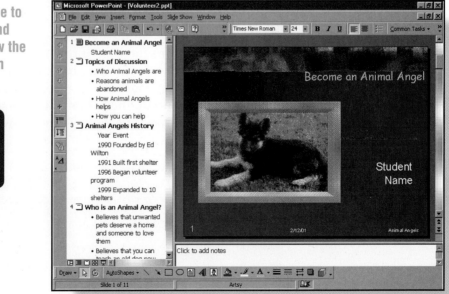

Figure 2–22

5 ━■ Switch to Slide Sorter view.

You can now see that the design has been applied all slides in the presentation.

Changing the Color Scheme

- -

As you look at the new design style, you feel the color is not very powerful. To make your presentation more lively, you decide to try a different color scheme. Each design template has several alternative color schemes from which you can choose. To see the color schemes that are available for the Artsy template,

1 ━■ Choose Format/Slide Color Scheme.

━■ If necessary, open the Standard tab.

Your screen should be similar to Figure 2–23.

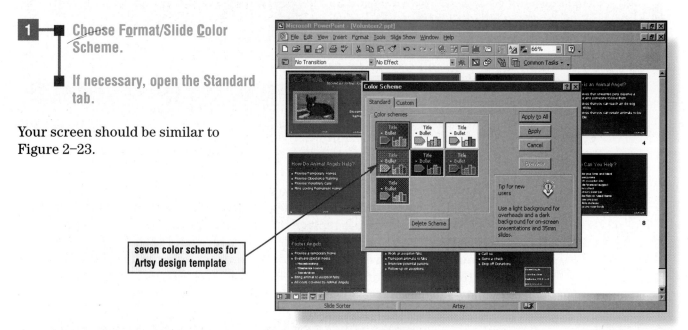

seven color schemes for Artsy design template

Figure 2–23

The seven color schemes for the Artsy design template are displayed. The color scheme with the gray background is selected. Each color scheme consists of eight coordinated colors that are applied to different slide elements. Using predefined color schemes gives your presentation a professional and consistent look. To see how the medium-blue color scheme would look,

2 Select the medium-blue color scheme option (first design, second row).

Click Preview .

If necessary, move the dialog box so you can see the slide in the workspace.

Your screen should be similar to Figure 2–24.

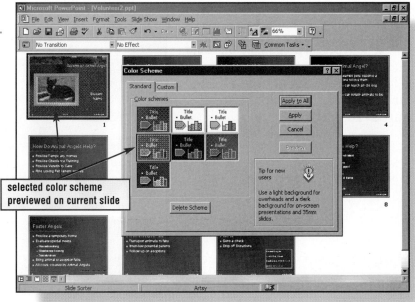

Figure 2–24

The current slide is displayed in the selected color scheme. Although you like this color scheme, you think the background looks too washed out, so you want to customize this scheme by changing the background color.

3 Open the Custom tab.

Your screen should be similar to Figure 2–25.

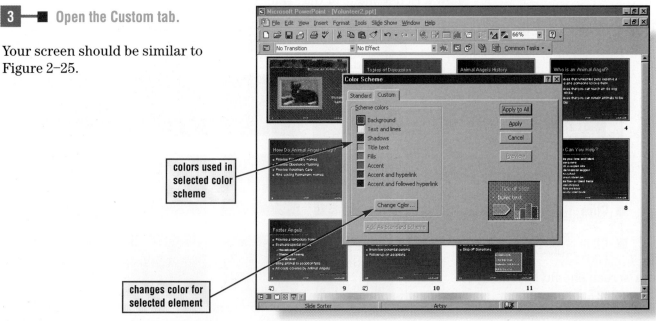

Figure 2–25

The Scheme Colors area of the dialog box shows you the eight colors that are applied to different elements of the template design. The sample box shows how the selected colors are used in a slide. The option to change the background color is selected by default. To select a different color for the background,

4   Click 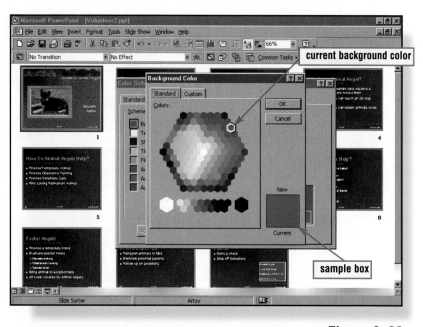.

· If necessary, open the Standard tab.

Your screen should be similar to Figure 2–26.

Figure 2–26

The dialog box displays a palette of standard colors. The current color of the background is selected. The sample box will show the new color you select in the upper half, and the current color in the lower half. Because you have not yet selected a new color, only one color is displayed. To see how a richer shade of the same color will look,

5   Select the color one up from the current selected color.

· Click   OK   .

· Click   Preview   .

· Click   Apply to All   .

Your screen should be similar to Figure 2–27.

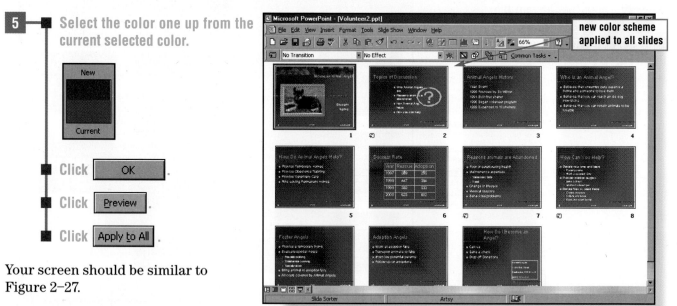

Figure 2–27

> The same procedure is used to change the colors of any other elements on the template.

The color background has changed on all slides in the presentation. This color gives the presentation much more impact.

6   To see how the changes you have made look when the slide is full screen, run the slide show.

As you ran the slide show, you may have noticed problems with how the custom slides you created adjusted when the new design template was applied.

For example, the table may no longer correctly display the contents. Before continuing, you want to make any necessary adjustments to the slides.

> **7** ■ Switch to Slide view.
>
> ■ Display slide 2 and, if necessary, move the placeholder for the text to the left and resize the clip art appropriately.
>
> ■ Display slide 6 and, if necessary, adjust the size of the table placeholder to fully display the headings on one line.

Modifying the Slide Master

While viewing the slide show, you think the slide appearance could be further improved by changing the font style of the bulleted text and the color of the title text. Although you can change each slide individually as you did in Tutorial 1, you can make the change much faster to all the slides by changing the slide master.

Concept Master

A **master** is a special slide that controls the format and placement of titles and text for all slides in your presentation. Each component of a presentation—title slide, slides, notes pages, and handout pages—has a corresponding master. The master contains formatted placeholders for the titles, main text, footnotes, background elements, and so on that appear on each associated slide or page. Any changes you make to a master affect all slides or pages associated with that master. The four masters are described below.

Master	Function
Slide Master	Defines the format and placement of the title and body text as well as the background of each slide in the presentation.
Title Master	Defines the format and placement of titles and text for slides that use the title layout.
Handout Master	Defines the format and placement of the slide image, text, headers, footers, and other elements that are to appear on every handout.
Notes Master	Defines the format and placement of the slide image, note text, headers, footers, and other elements that are to appear on all speaker notes.

If you modify the text color, font style, or size of slide titles on the slide master, all slides in the presentation will change accordingly. Likewise, if you add a graphic such as a company logo to the slide master, it will appear on every slide. However, if you modify the format or layout of the title master, only those slides that you have designated as title slides will change. Each design template comes with its own slide master. When you apply a new design template to a presentation, all slides and masters are updated to those of the new design template.

You can create slides that differ from the master by changing the format and placement of elements in the individual slide rather than on the master. For example, when you change the font of a title on a single slide, the slide master is not affected. Only the individual slide reflects the change, making it unique. If you have created a unique slide, the elements you changed on that slide retain their uniqueness even if you later make changes to the slide master, including changing the design template.

Using the master to modify or add elements to a presentation ensures consistency and saves time.

Each master is displayed in its own view. To display the slide master,

1 Choose View/Master/Slide Master.

> You also can hold down ⇧Shift and click ⬜ Slide View to display the slide master.

Your screen should be similar to Figure 2–28.

> The Master toolbar may also be displayed.

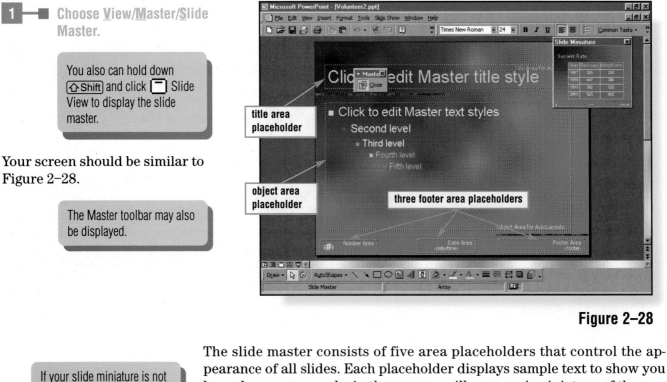

Figure 2–28

The slide master consists of five area placeholders that control the appearance of all slides. Each placeholder displays sample text to show you how changes you make in these areas will appear. A miniature of the current slide is also displayed to show you how changes you make to the master slide will affect the presentation.

> If your slide miniature is not displayed, choose View/Slide Miniature.

First you will change the font color of the title text.

2 Click the title area.

Click ⬛ Font Color and select orange.

> The font color palette displays colors from the selected color scheme.

Your screen should be similar to Figure 2–29.

Figure 2–29

All the sample title text in the placeholder, as well as the title in the slide miniature, changed to the new color. Next you want to change the font style of the bulleted text in the object area.

Select the first two levels of bulleted heads in the object area and change the font style to Times New Roman.

Your screen should be similar to Figure 2–30.

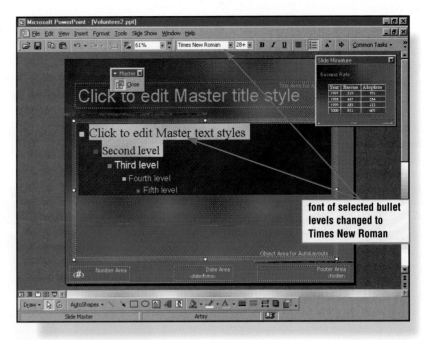

Figure 2–30

Finally, you decide to delete the date from the footer.

4 Select the Date Area placeholder.

Press Delete.

The Date Area placeholder is removed. To better see how the changes you have made to the slide master affected the slides,

 Click ☐ Slide View.

Display slide 7.

Your screen should be similar to Figure 2–31.

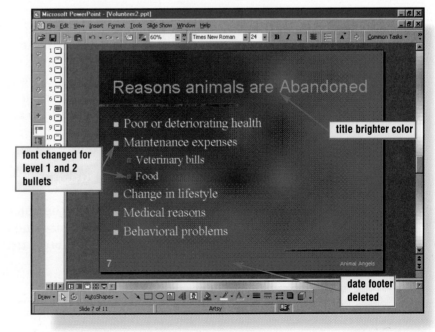

Figure 2–31

The title color change and bulleted font style changes you made are now easy to see.

6 ■ Switch to Slide Sorter view.

You can now see that all slides in the presentation have been modified. The changes to the two levels of bulleted text are reflected in all slides containing those level heads. None of the slides, except the title slide, displays the date in the footer.

You think several slides that do not have much text would look better with the point size increased to 36 pt.

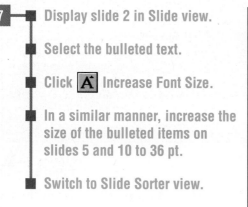

7 ■ Display slide 2 in Slide view.

■ Select the bulleted text.

■ Click $\boxed{A}$ Increase Font Size.

■ In a similar manner, increase the size of the bulleted items on slides 5 and 10 to 36 pt.

■ Switch to Slide Sorter view.

Your screen should be similar to Figure 2–32.

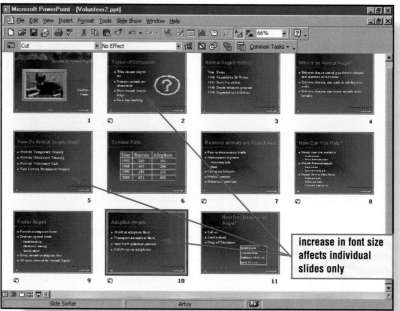

Figure 2–32

The changes you have made to these slides using the $\boxed{A}$ button affect the current slide only, making them unique slides in the presentation. The slide master is not changed. If you now changed the first-level bulleted text on the slide master, the first-level text on these slides would not be affected, because changes made to an individual slide override the master slide.

Modifying the Title Master

Next you want to enhance the appearance of the title slide master. First you will increase the font size and add a shadow and italics to the title. Then you will change the subtitle text to a different color with a shadow.

1 Display slide 1 in Slide view.

Hold down ⇧Shift and click ⬒ Slide View.

> The menu equivalent is **V**iew/**M**aster/**T**itle Master.

Click the master title text placeholder.

Your screen should be similar to Figure 2–33.

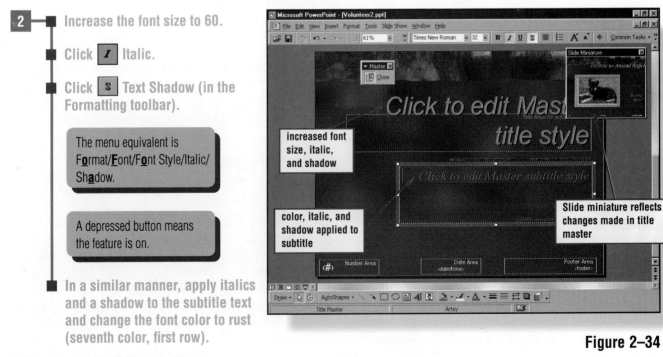

Figure 2–33

Notice the title master has a slightly different appearance from the title slide in your presentation. This is because you modified the title slide by moving placeholders and changing the font, size, and color, making it a unique slide. The unique changes you made to that slide were not changed when the title master of the Artsy design template was applied. The title master attributes reflect the attributes associated with the Artsy template, such as the title font of Arial, 44 pt as shown in the toolbar buttons as well as the original layout.

2 Increase the font size to 60.

Click *I* Italic.

Click **S** Text Shadow (in the Formatting toolbar).

> The menu equivalent is **F**ormat/**F**ont/**Fo**nt Style/Italic/Sh**a**dow.

> A depressed button means the feature is on.

In a similar manner, apply italics and a shadow to the subtitle text and change the font color to rust (seventh color, first row).

Your screen should be similar to Figure 2–34.

Figure 2–34

Although the miniature displays the changes, it is difficult to see. To see how the title slide looks with the changes you have made,

3 ▬ ■ Switch to Slide view.

Your screen should be similar to Figure 2–35.

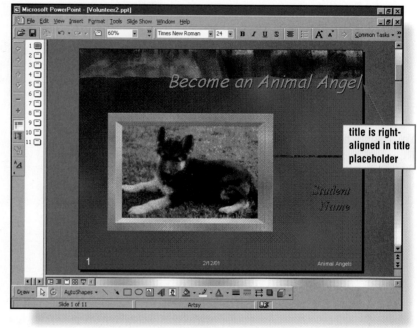

Figure 2–35

The title is still not how you want it to appear. It is too far to the right edge of the screen. You could move the placeholder to position the text, or you can change the alignment of the entry in the placeholder. Currently, the title is right-aligned. You will change the alignment to left and move the placeholder down so the title does not touch the top border graphic.

4 ▬ ■ Select the title placeholder.

■ Click 📊 Align Left.

■ Drag the placeholder down slightly until the title appears as in Figure 2–36.

Your screen should be similar to Figure 2–36.

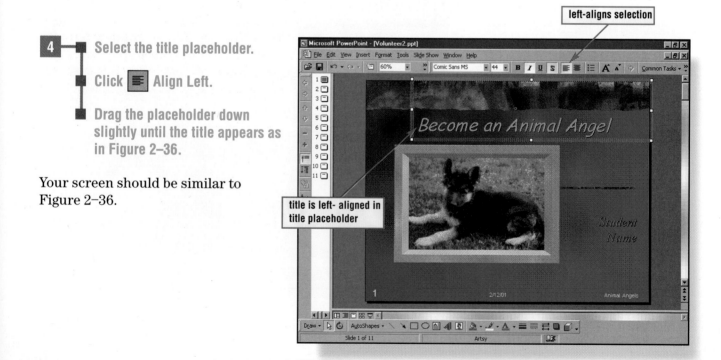

Figure 2-36

Hiding the Title Slide Footer

You would also like to not display the footer information on the title slide. To turn off the display of this information,

1 Choose **V**iew/**H**eader and Footer.

   Open the Slide tab, if necessary.

Your screen should be similar to Figure 2–37.

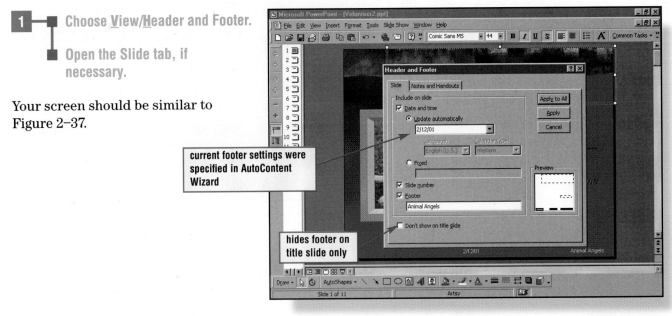

Figure 2–37

When you created the presentation using the AutoContent Wizard, many of the footer options were specified at that time. The Header and Footer dialog box displays those settings. The Date and Time option is selected, and the date is set to update automatically using the current system date whenever the presentation is opened. You can also change this option to enter a fixed date that will not change. Additionally, the slide number was preselected, and the text you entered, Animal Angels, appears in the footer text box. You could turn off these options and delete the footer text in order to remove this information from the current slide. Because it is very common to not display this information on a title slide, there is an option to hide it for that type of slide.

2 ■ Select Don't show on title slide.

■ Click [Apply].

Additional Information

The [Apply] command button applies the current settings to the selected slides only. Using [Apply to All] applies the current setting to the entire presentation, including the corresponding master.

Your screen should be similar to Figure 2–38.

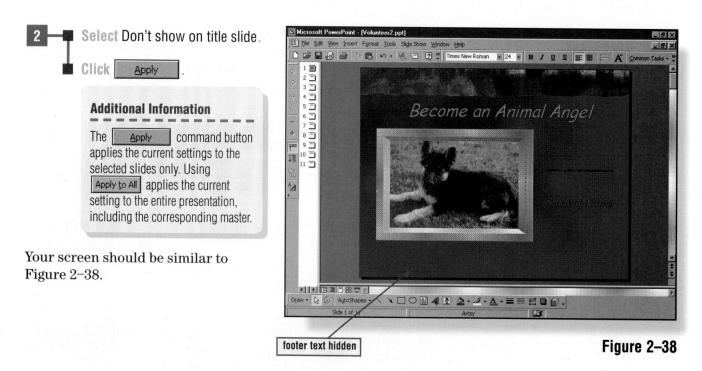

footer text hidden

Figure 2–38

You have made many changes to the presentation. To see how they will look when the presentation is run,

1 ■ Click 🖵 Slide Show.

■ Click on each slide to advance through the presentation.

You think the presentation looks pretty good, but have several changes in mind to make it more interesting. For example, you want to add a concluding slide to mark the end of the presentation, and you want to include several features that will animate the presentation.

Note: If you are ending your session now, save the presentation as Final Volunteer and exit PowerPoint. When you begin again, open this file.

Duplicating a Slide

Every presentation should have a concluding slide. To create the concluding slide, you will duplicate slide 1. Duplicating a slide creates a copy of the selected slide and places it directly after the selected slide. You can duplicate a slide in any view, but in this case you will use the outline pane in Slide view. To duplicate slide 1 and move it to the end of the presentation,

1 ■ Click ⊟ slide 1 in the outline pane.

■ Choose **I**nsert/**D**uplicate Slide.

■ Click and drag ⊟ slide 2 in the outline pane to the end of the list of slides.

■ Click in the subtitle placeholder and replace your name with **The End**.

Your screen should be similar to Figure 2–39.

> You can also duplicate a slide using the Copy and Paste commands on the Edit menu.

Figure 2–39

Creating a Drawing Object

The concluding slide in the presentation needs to be more powerful. This is your last chance to convince your audience to help the Animal Angels organization. You decide to add a graphic of a heart in place of the picture. To quickly add a shape, you will use one of the ready-made shapes supplied with PowerPoint called **AutoShapes.** These include such basic shapes as rectangles and circles, a variety of lines, block arrows, flowchart symbols, stars and banners, and callouts.

1 ■ Select the frame and press
[Delete]

■ In a similar manner, delete the
picture.

■ Click AutoShapes ▾ .

■ Select **B**asic Shapes.

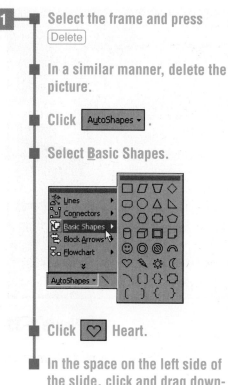

■ Click ♡ Heart.

■ In the space on the left side of
the slide, click and drag down-
ward and to the right to create
the heart.

> The menu equivalent is
> **I**nsert/**P**icture/**A**utoShapes.

Your screen should be similar to
Figure 2–40.

> To maintain the height and width
> proportions of the AutoShape, hold
> down [⇧ Shift] while you drag.

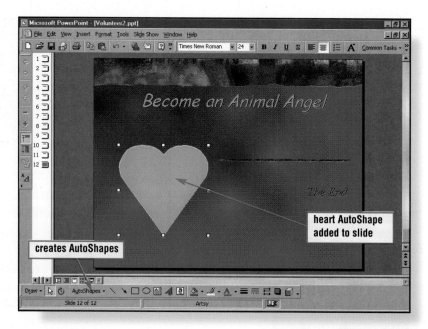

Figure 2–40

The AutoShape graphic object you selected is inserted into the document.
It can be sized and moved just like any other object.

2 ■ If necessary, size and position the heart as in Figure 2–40 above.

Enhancing Drawing Objects

Next you will add text to the object and enhance its appearance using several features on the Drawing toolbar.

1 Right-click on the AutoShape object to open the shortcut menu, and select Add Text.

Change the font to Arial and bold.

Type **Open Your Heart**.

Your screen should be similar to Figure 2–41.

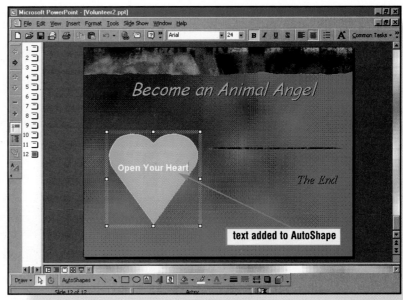

Figure 2–41

Next you will add a shadow behind the heart. Then you will change the color of the shadow so it is easier to see.

2 Click Shadow and select any shadow style from the pop-up menu.

Click 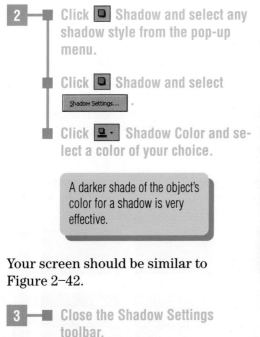 Shadow and select Shadow Settings... .

Click 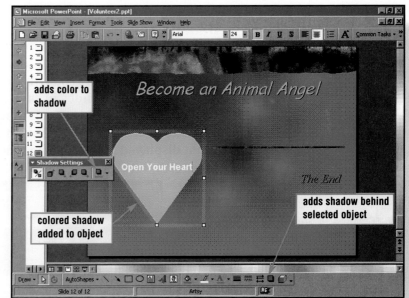 Shadow Color and select a color of your choice.

> A darker shade of the object's color for a shadow is very effective.

Your screen should be similar to Figure 2–42.

Figure 2–42

3 Close the Shadow Settings toolbar.

> The rotate handles are small circles on each corner of the selected object.

Finally, you want to change the angle of the object. You can rotate an object 90 degrees left or right, or to any other angle. You will change the angle of the heart to the right using the Free Rotate feature. This feature displays handles called **rotate handles** for the selected object, which allow you to rotate the object to any degree in any direction. Holding down ⇧Shift while using the Free Rotate tool rotates the object in 15-degree increments.

4 Click **⟳** Free Rotate.

Hold down ⇧Shift while you drag the lower right corner rotate handle to the right one increment.

Your screen should be similar to Figure 2–43.

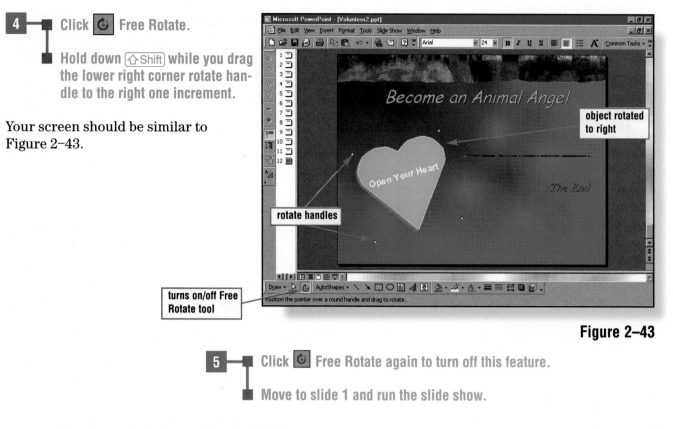

Figure 2–43

5 Click **⟳** Free Rotate again to turn off this feature.

Move to slide 1 and run the slide show.

Hiding Slides

As you reconsider the presentation, you decide to show the Success slide only if someone asks about this information. To do this, you will hide the slide. You can hide slides in several views, but the procedure is easiest in Slide Sorter view. Slide Sorter view also has its own toolbar that makes it easy to perform many different tasks in this view. The Formatting toolbar is not displayed because you cannot format slides in this view.

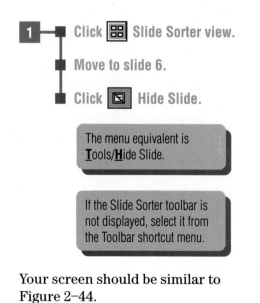

1 Click **⊞** Slide Sorter view.

Move to slide 6.

Click **▣** Hide Slide.

The menu equivalent is **T**ools/**H**ide Slide.

If the Slide Sorter toolbar is not displayed, select it from the Toolbar shortcut menu.

Your screen should be similar to Figure 2–44.

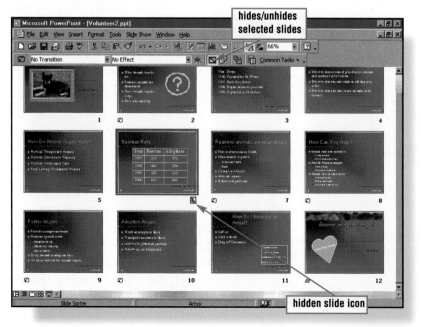

Figure 2–44

Notice that the slide number for slide 6 is surrounded by a box with a slash drawn through it. This indicates that the slide is hidden. Next you will run the slide show to see how hidden slides work. You will begin the show at the slide before the hidden slide.

2 ■ Select slide 5.

   ■ Run the slide show.

   ■ Display the next slide, which should be Reasons Animals are Abandoned.

Slide 6 was not displayed because it is hidden. To show how to display a hidden slide, you will return to slide 5 and then display slide 6.

> The command to display a hidden slide is <u>G</u>o/By <u>T</u>itle on the shortcut menu. H is the keyboard shortcut.

3 ■ Press Pg Up.

   ■ Press the letter H to see slide 6.

   ■ Continue the slide show until you are returned to Slide Sorter view.

> The H is not case sensitive.

Animating Objects and Adding Sound Effects

Next you would like to use some of PowerPoint's special effects to enhance the onscreen presentation.

Concept ⑤ Special Effects

Special effects such as animation, sound, slide transitions, and build slides are used to enhance an onscreen presentation.

   Animation adds action to text and graphics so they move around on the screen. You can assign sounds to further enhance the effect.

   Transitions control how one slide moves off the screen and the next one appears. You can select from many different transition choices. You may choose Dissolve for your title slide to give it an added flair. After that you could use Wipe Right for all the slides until the next to the last, and then use Dissolve again to end the show. As with any special effect, use slide transitions carefully.

   Builds are used to display each bullet point, text, paragraph, or graphic independently of the other text or objects on the slide. You set up the way you want each element to appear (to fly in from the left, for instance) and whether you want the other elements already on the slide to dim or shimmer when a new element is added. For example, since your audience is used to reading from left to right, you could design your build slides so the bullet points fly in from the left. Then, when you want to emphasize a point, bring a bullet point in from the right. That change grabs the audience's attention.

   When you present a slide show, the content of your presentation should take center stage. You want the special effects you use, such as animation, builds, and transitions, to help emphasize the main points in your presentation—not draw the audience's attention to the special effects.

To further enhance the AutoShape object on the final slide, you will add two special effects, a custom animation and sound, to this object.

1 ■ Move to slide 12.

■ Switch to Slide view.

■ Right-click on the AutoShape object to open the shortcut menu, and select Custo**m** Animation.

■ If necessary, open the Effects tab.

Your screen should be similar to Figure 2–45.

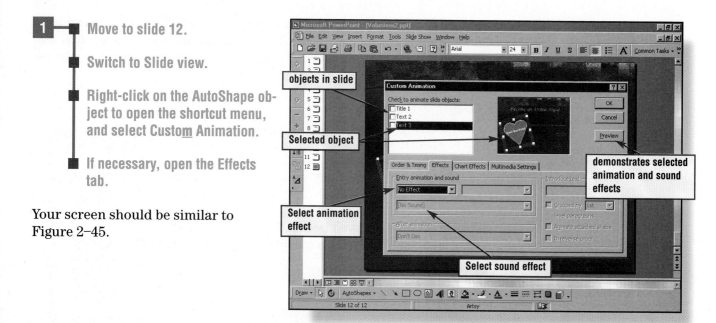

Figure 2–45

All three objects on the slide are listed, and the preview shows the AutoShape object is selected. You could assign animations and sound to all three objects on the slide and also determine the order in which they display. You will animate the AutoShape object only.

2 ■ In the Check to Animate Slide Objects list box, select Text 3.

■ From the Entry Animation drop-down lists, select Dissolve as the animation and Chime as the sound effect.

■ Click Preview to see a demonstration of the selected animation and sound effect.

■ Click OK .

> You must have a speaker and a sound card to hear the sound.

Next you want to see how the animation will work while the presentation is running. When you run a slide show, it will begin at the current slide location. Also, you need to click on the slide to activate the animation and sound effect.

3 ■ Click  Slide Show.

■ Click the slide.

Slide 12 is displayed in Slide Show view and, after you clicked on the slide, the heart appeared using the dissolve effect and the chime sound played. You can end a slide show at any point by pressing (Esc), and the slide you are viewing becomes the current slide.

4 ■ Press (Esc) to end the slide show.

Adding Transition Effects

You would like to add a transition effect to the slides.

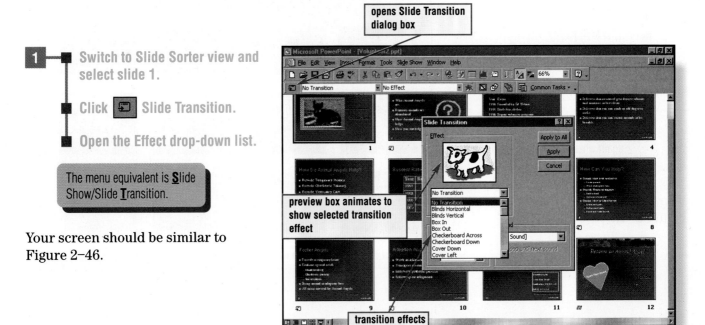

Figure 2–46

1 Switch to Slide Sorter view and select slide 1.

Click  Slide Transition.

Open the Effect drop-down list.

The menu equivalent is **S**lide Show/Slide **T**ransition.

Your screen should be similar to Figure 2–46.

The Effect drop-down list box displays the names of the transition effects that can be used on the slides. Currently No Transition is selected. The preview box will show how the selected transition effects work as they are selected from the list.

Using ↑ and ↓ to move the highlight in the list box selects the effect and leaves the list open so you can preview others.

2 Press ↓.

Select a few of the other transition effects to see how they work.

You decide to try the Wipe Right transition effect on this slide.

> **3** ■ Scroll the list box and select **Wipe Right**.
>
> ■ Click **Apply**.

Additional Information

You can click the preview box to watch the selected transition effect again when the Effect list is closed.

Your screen should be similar to Figure 2–47.

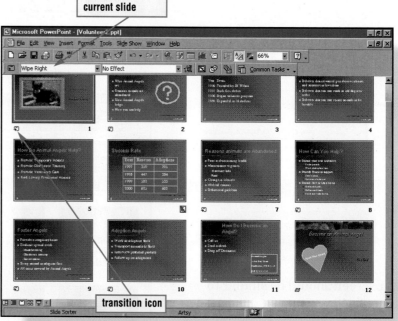

Figure 2–47

A preview of the selected transition effect is displayed on the slide in Slide Sorter view, and a transition icon is displayed below slide 1. This indicates that a transition effect has been applied to the slide. Also notice that the Wipe Right Slide Transition Effects button displays the name of the effect applied to the selected slide. Several other slides in the presentation also display a transition effect icon. This is because the AutoContent Wizard automatically used the Cut transition effect on all slides, except the title slide, that were added when the presentation was created originally.

> **4** ■ Run the slide show.
>
> ■ Press Esc after viewing a few slides.

You like how the transition effect works and decide to use the Random Transition effect, which will randomly select different transition effects, on all the slides. To select and change all the slides at once,

5   Choose Edit/Select All.

The keyboard shortcut is
Ctrl + A.

Click
Slide Transition Effects.

Choose Random Transition (last
option in Effects drop-down list).

Additional Information

Using the Slide Transition Effects
button does not display the Slide
Transition dialog box, and it cannot
be used to preview the effects.

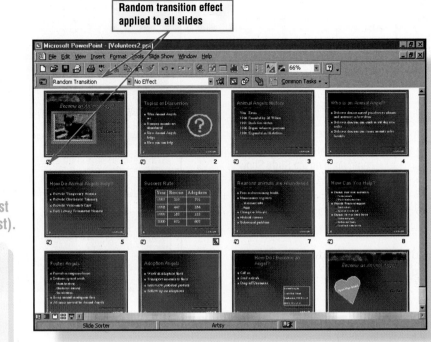

Figure 2–48

Your screen should be similar to
Figure 2–48.

The transition icon appears below each slide, indicating that a transition
effect has been applied to all slides.

6   Run the slide show from the beginning to see the different effects.

Adding Build Effects

The next effect you want to add to the slides is a build to progressively display each bullet on a slide. When a build is applied to a slide, the slide initially shows only the title. The bulleted text appears as the presentation
proceeds. A build slide can also include different build transition effects,
which are similar to slide transition effects. The effect is applied to the
bulleted text as it is displayed on the slide.

Additional Information

You can select and deselect multiple slides by holding down Ctrl
while making your selection.

You would like to add a build to all slides in the presentation except
slides 1, 3, 6, and 12. Because all slides are still selected, you need to deselect the four slides only. To do this, hold down Ctrl while clicking on the
slide.

1   Deselect slides 1, 3, 6, and 12.

Now, to add a build to all the selected slides and use the Fly From Left
build transition effect,

2 ■ Click No Effect ▾ Preset Animation.

■ Choose Fly From Left.

Additional Information

You can also use the **P**reset Animation and Custo**m** Animation commands on the Sli**d**e Show menu to add sound build effects. To use this option, you must be in Slide view.

Your screen should be similar to Figure 2–49.

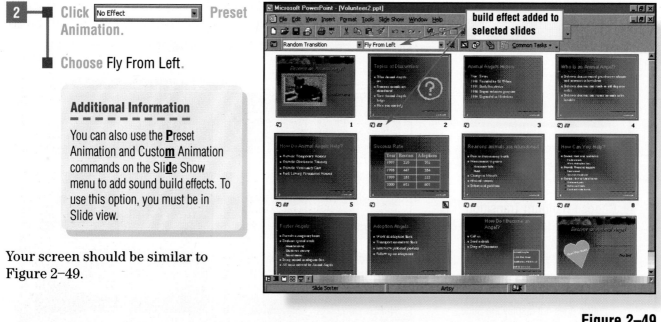

Figure 2–49

A preview of the selected build effect is displayed on the current slide in Slide Sorter view, and the 🗗 Build icon is displayed below the selected slides, indicating they are build slides. The Preset Animation button shows the selected build effect.

Now that you have added the transition and build, you would like to see how they affect the slide show.

3 ■ Select slide 1 and run the slide show.

■ Move to the next slide.

Your screen should be similar to Figure 2–50.

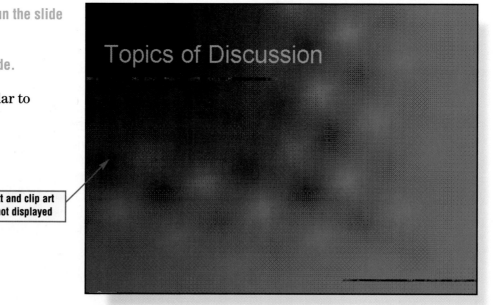

bulleted text and clip art object are not displayed

Figure 2–50

The second slide is displayed using a transition effect, but does not display any of the bulleted items. When a build is applied to a slide, the objects and bulleted items are displayed only when you click or use any of the procedures to advance to the next slide. This allows the presenter to focus the audience's attention and to control the pace of the presentation. The build effect displays the bulleted text using the Fly From Left build transition effects.

4 ▬■ To display the bulleted items and the clip art object, click or press Spacebar five times.

Your screen should be similar to Figure 2–51.

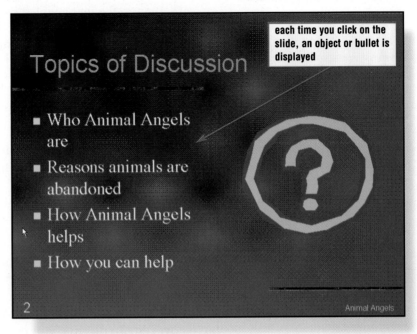

Figure 2–51

Controlling the Slide Show

As much as you would like to control a presentation, the presence of an audience usually causes the presentation to change course. PowerPoint has several ways you can control a slide show during the presentation. Before presenting a slide show, you should rehearse the presentation. To help with this aspect of the presentation, PowerPoint includes a Rehearse Timings option on the Slide Show menu that records the time you spend on each slide as you practice your narration. If your computer is set up with a microphone, you could even record your narration with the Record Narration option. Running the slide show and practicing how to control the slide show helps you have a smooth presentation. To try out some of the features you can use while running the slide show,

1 ▬■ Click or press Spacebar until the title of slide 5 appears.

Slide 5 should be displayed. If someone has a question about a previous slide, you can go backward and redisplay it.

2 ▬■ Press Backspace five times.

You returned the onscreen presentation to slide 3. But now, because the audience already viewed slide 4, you want to advance to slide 5. To go to a specific slide number, you type the slide number and press ←Enter.

You also can choose **G**o/Slide **N**avigator from the shortcut menu to select a slide to move to.

3 Press **5**.

Press [←Enter].

Display the four bulleted items on slide 5.

Sometimes an audience member may get the entire presentation off-track. If you find yourself on another topic altogether, you can black out the screen. To do this,

The menu equivalent is **S**creen/ **B**lack Screen on the shortcut menu.

4 Press **B**.

The B is not case sensitive.

The screen goes to black while you address the topic. When you are ready to resume the presentation, to bring the slide back,

5 Press **B**.

Adding Freehand Annotations

During your presentation, you may want to point to an important word, underline an important point, or draw checkmarks next to items that you have covered. To do this, you can use the mouse pointer during the presentation.

1 To display the mouse pointer, move the mouse pointer on the screen.

In its current shape  , you can use the mouse pointer to point to items on the slide. You can also use it to draw on the screen by changing the pointer to a pen, which activates the freehand annotation feature.

2 Right-click to display the short-cut menu.

Choose P**o**inter Options.

Your screen should be similar to Figure 2–52.

You can also click the button that appears in the lower left corner of the slide when you move the mouse to open the shortcut menu.

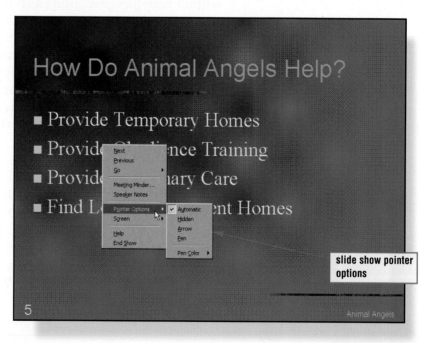

Figure 2–52

The default option, Automatic, automatically hides the slide show pointer if it is not moved for 15 seconds. It appears again when you move the mouse pointer. The other options are described in the following table.

Option	Effect
Arrow	Displays the pointer as an arrow and does not hide it.
Hidden	Hides the pointer until another pointer option is selected.
Pen	Changes the pointer to a pen and turns on freehand annotation. You can also use Pen Color to turn on the annotation and specify the color of line to draw.

The keyboard shortcut is [Ctrl] + P.

3 ■ Select **P**en.

The mouse pointer changes to a ✎. To see how the freehand annotation feature works, you will underline the last bullet. To draw, you drag the pen pointer in the direction you want to draw.

4 ■ Move the mouse pointer under the Find Loving Permanent Homes.

■ Drag the pen pointer until the underline is drawn.

To draw a straight line, hold down [⇧ Shift] while dragging.

Your screen should be similar to Figure 2–53.

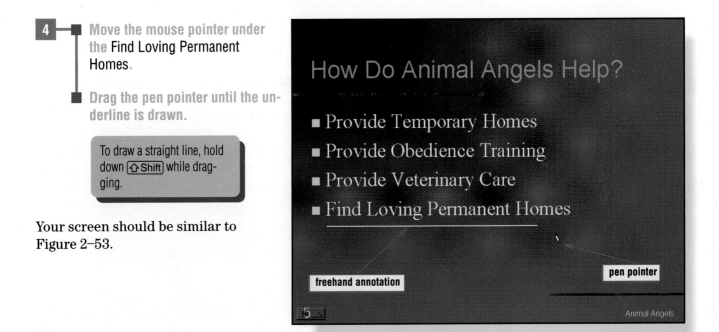

Figure 2–53

5 Practice using the freehand annotator to draw any shapes you want on the slide.

To turn off the freehand annotation feature, select Pointer Options/Automatic from the shortcut menu.

> You can also erase annotations by selecting Screen/Erase Pen from the shortcut menu. The keyboard shortcut is E.

The mouse pointer shape returns to a ☖. You do not have to be concerned about cluttering your slides with freehand drawings because they are erased when you continue the presentation.

6 Press Esc to end the slide show.

Creating Speaker Notes

When making your presentation, there are some critical points you want to be sure to discuss. To help you remember the important points, you can use **notes pages.** These pages show a miniature of the slide and provide an area to enter speaker notes. You can create notes pages for some or all of the slides in a presentation. Notes pages can also be used to remind you of hidden slides. You decide to create speaker notes on slide 5 to remind you about the hidden slide.

1 Switch to Normal view.

Display slide 5.

Click in the Notes pane.

Your screen should be similar to Figure 2–54.

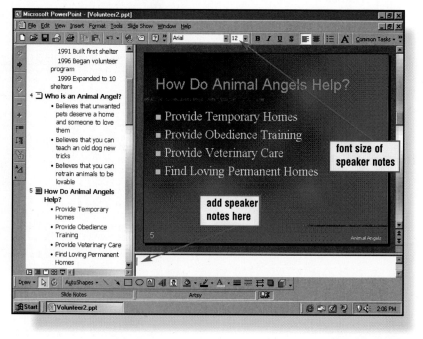

Figure 2–54

Notice that the Font Size button shows the current font size is 12 pt. To make the speaker notes easy to read in a dimly lit room while you are making the presentation, you would like to use a larger type size.

Increase the font size to 24.

Type **Show the next hidden slide if someone asks about how many animals are adopted**.

Your screen should be similar to Figure 2-55.

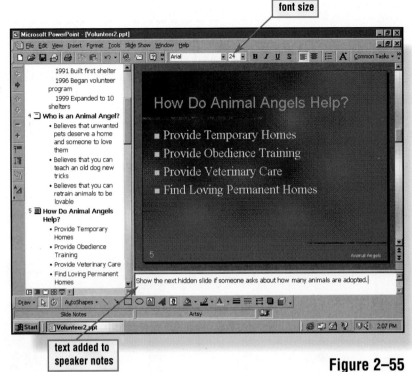

Figure 2-55

Although the text does not appear in 24-point size, it will print that way. To see how the notes page will look when printed,

 Choose <u>V</u>iew/ Notes <u>P</u>age.

Your screen should be similar to Figure 2-56.

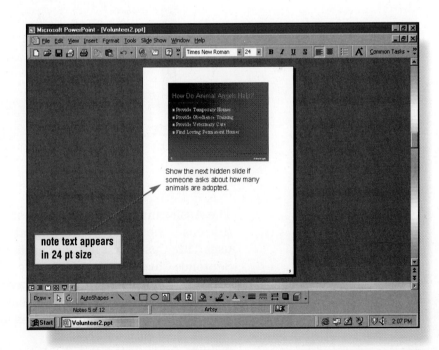

Figure 2-56

Checking the Style

You want to use the Style Checker to make a final check for consistency and style. The Style Checker is only active when the Office Assistant is displayed. It displays a lightbulb on any slides in which it detects a potential problem.

> If your school has disabled the Office Assistant, you will not be able to complete this section.

> **Additional Information**
>
> You can change the style options that are checked using **T**ools/ **O**ptions/Spelling and Style/**S**tyle Options.

1 ■ Display slide 1 in Normal view.

■ Turn on the Office Assistant.

■ Move to slide 2.

■ Click on the lightbulb.

Your screen should be similar to Figure 2–57.

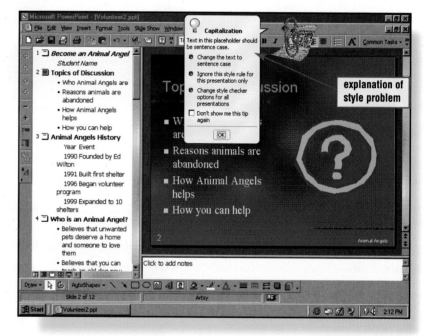

Figure 2–57

The Assistant displays an explanation of the problem it has located. In this case, the problem is a capitalization error. The default slide design uses Title Case (first letter of each word is capitalized) for slide titles and Sentence Case (first letter of sentence is capitalized) for body text. No end punctuation is used. However, leaving the body text style option selected will change proper names, such as the name of the agency, to lowercase. To turn off this option for this presentation only,

2 ■ Select Ignore this style rule for this presentation only.

The lightbulb is cleared from the slide.

3 ■ Click on the lightbulb on slide 4 next.

■ Select Change the text to title case.

■ If a lightbulb appears on slide 6, click on it.

In this case, there is a suggestion to add to the slide a clip art graphic that represents success. To continue without following the suggestion,

4 ■ Click OK.

■ Click the lightbulb on slide 7.

■ Select Change the text to title case.

■ Click the lightbulb on slide 8.

Your screen should be similar to Figure 2–58.

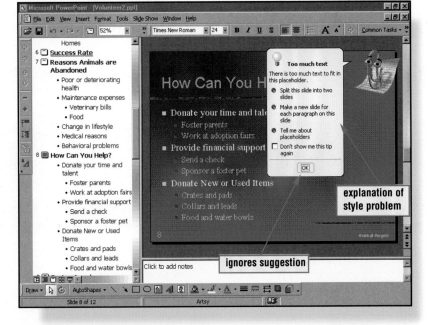

Figure 2–58

The problem identified in this slide is that there is too much text for the slide. When a style check is made, each slide is examined for visual clarity. The default settings use guidelines for proper slide design: the font size is large, the number of fonts used is small, and the amount of text on a slide is limited. All these settings help you adhere to good slide design. In this case, however, you feel the slide looks all right as is. To ignore the suggestions and proceed,

5 ■ Click OK.

Choose **O**ptions from the Assistant shortcut menu and clear the Use the Office Assistant check box in the Options tab.

■ Continue through the rest of the presentation and correct any style issues you feel are necessary.

■ Turn off the Office Assistant.

Documenting a File

You will save the completed presentation in a new file named Final Volunteer. In addition, you want to include file documentation with the file when it is saved. To do this,

1 ■— Choose File/Properties.

■ Open the Summary tab if necessary.

Your screen should be similar to Figure 2–59.

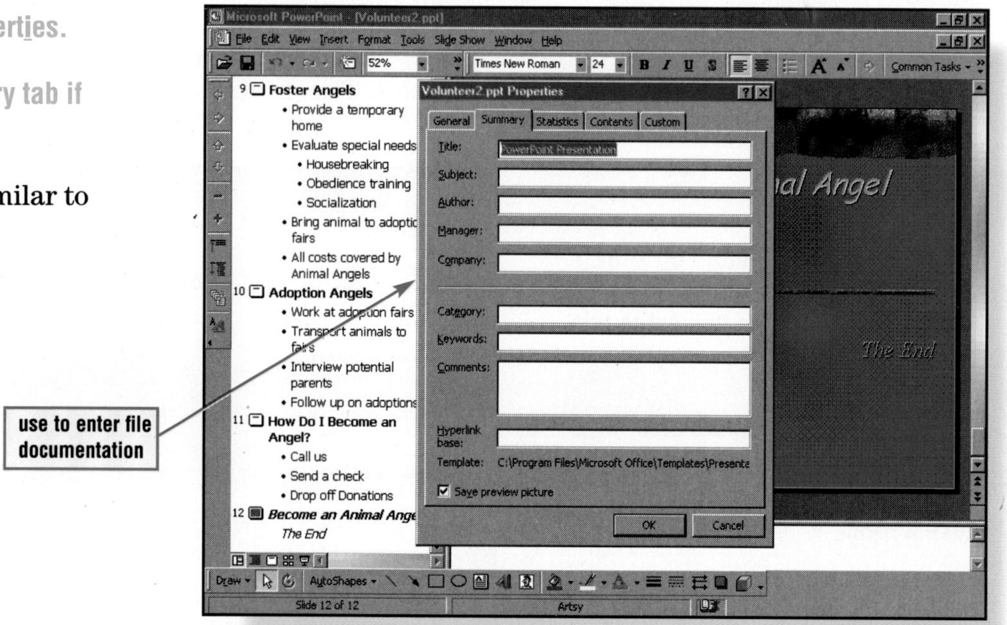

use to enter file documentation

Figure 2–59

The Summary tab text boxes are used for the following:

Option	Action
Title	Enter the presentation title. This title can be longer and more descriptive than the presentation file name.
Subject	Enter a description of the presentation's content.
Author	Enter the name of the presentation's author. By default this is the name entered when PowerPoint was installed.
Manager	Enter the name of your manager.
Company	Enter the name of your company.
Category	Enter the name of a higher-level category under which you can group similar types of presentations.
Keywords	Enter words that you associate with the presentation so the Find File command can be used.
Comments	Enter any comments you feel are appropriate for the presentation.
Hyperbase link	Enter the path or URL that you want to use for all hyperlinks in the document.
Template	Identifies the template that is attached to the file.

If you press ⟮←Enter⟯, the ⟮ OK ⟯ button will be selected and the dialog box will close. To re-open the Summary Info dialog box, choose **F**ile/Proper**ti**es.

2 ■ In the title text box, enter **Animal Angels**.

■ In the subject text box, enter **Volunteer recruitment**.

■ In the Author text box, enter **your name**.

■ Click ⟮ OK ⟯.

Printing Notes Pages and Selected Slides

You have created both slides and notes pages for the presentation. To print the notes pages on which you entered text,

1 ■ Choose **F**ile/**P**rint/Print **w**hat/Notes Pages.

■ From the Print Range area, select **S**lides.

■ Type **5**.

■ Click ⟮ OK ⟯.

The notes pages should be printing. Next you will print a few selected slides to be used as handouts.

2 ■ Choose **F**ile/**P**rint/Print **w**hat/Handouts.

■ Specify 3 slides per page.

■ Select **S**lides.

■ Type **1, 2, 6, 11, 12**.

To scale the slides to fit the paper in your printer, and to add a thin border around the slides as a frame,

3 ■ Select Scale to **F**it Paper.

■ If necessary, select Fra**m**e Slides.

■ Click ⟮ OK ⟯.

The view you are in when saving the file is the view that will be displayed when the file is opened.

■ Save the completed presentation file as **Final Volunteer**.

■ Exit PowerPoint.

Concept Summary

Tutorial 2: Modifying and Refining a Presentation

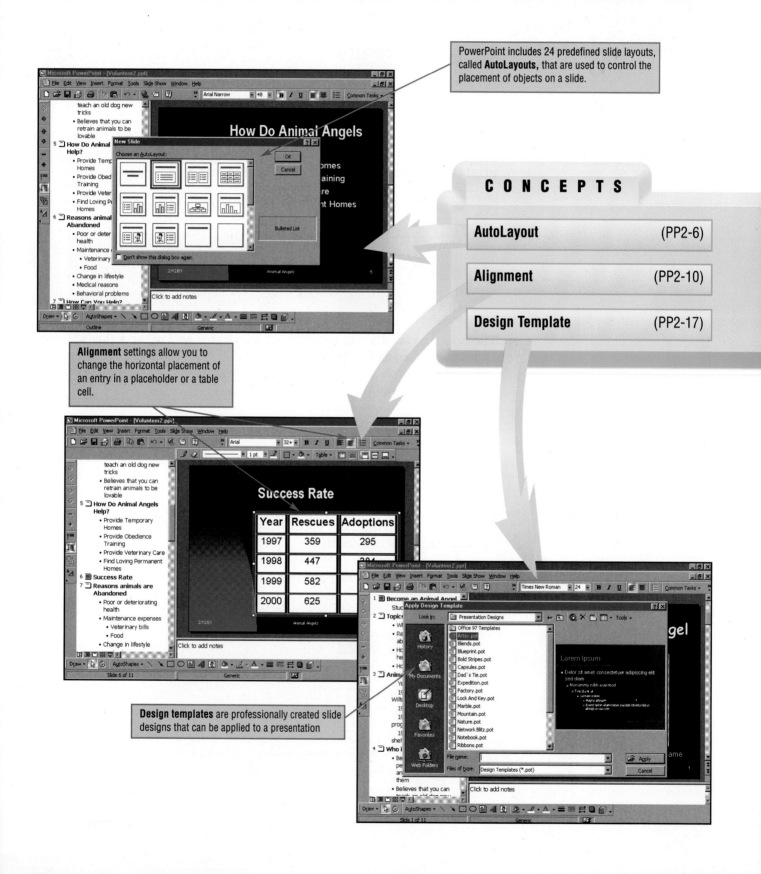

PowerPoint includes 24 predefined slide layouts, called **AutoLayouts,** that are used to control the placement of objects on a slide.

C O N C E P T S

AutoLayout	(PP2-6)
Alignment	(PP2-10)
Design Template	(PP2-17)

Alignment settings allow you to change the horizontal placement of an entry in a placeholder or a table cell.

Design templates are professionally created slide designs that can be applied to a presentation

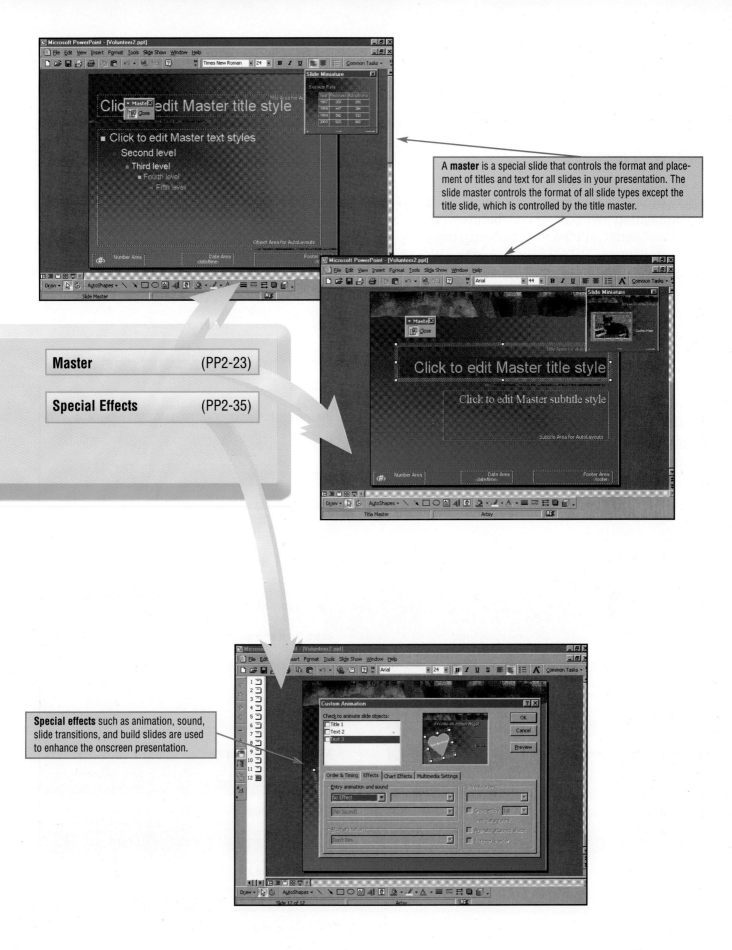

A **master** is a special slide that controls the format and placement of titles and text for all slides in your presentation. The slide master controls the format of all slide types except the title slide, which is controlled by the title master.

Master (PP2-23)

Special Effects (PP2-35)

Special effects such as animation, sound, slide transitions, and build slides are used to enhance the onscreen presentation.

Tutorial Review

Key Terms

alignment PP2-10	attribute PP2-8	notes page PP2-45
animation PP2-35	builds PP2-35	rotate handle PP2-33
AutoLayout PP2-6	design template PP2-17	style PP2-8
AutoShapes PP2-31	master PP2-23	transitions PP2-35

Command Summary

Command	Shortcut Keys	Button	Action
File/Properties			Displays statistics and stores information about the presentation
Edit/Find	Ctrl + F		Finds selected text
Edit/Replace	Ctrl + H		Replaces selected text
View/Notes Page			Displays notes pages
View/Master/Slide Master	⇧Shift + ☐		Displays slide master for current presentation
View/Master/Title Master			Displays title master for current presentation
View/Header and Footer			Specifies information that appears as headers and footers on slides, notes, outlines, and handout pages
Insert/Duplicate Slide			Inserts duplicate of selected slide.
Insert/Picture/AutoShapes			Inserts selected AutoShape object
Insert/text Box		🖾	Adds a text box.
Format/Font/Font Style/Bold		**B**	Adds bold effect to selection
Format/Font/Font Style/Italic		*I*	Adds italics effects to selection
Format/Font/Shadow			Adds shadow effect to selection
Format/Font/Color		**A** ⋅	Adds color to selection
Format/Alignment		≡ ≡ ≡ ≡	Left, center, right aligns, or justifies each line in a cell or placeholder.
Format/Slide Layout			Changes or creates a slide layout
Format/Slide Color Scheme			Changes color scheme of one or all slides in presentation
Format/Background			Changes color of slide background
Format/Apply Design Template		🔖	Changes appearance of slide by applying a different design template

Command	Shortcut Keys	Button	Action
Format/Picture/Recolor		🖼	Sets color and style options
Tools/Options/Spelling and Style			Sets spelling and style options
Slide Show/Hide Slide		▣	Hides selected slide
Slide Show/Preset Animation		No Effect ▾	Adds builds to selected slides
Slide Show/Slide Transition		▤	Adds transition effects
Slide Show Shortcut Menu			
Go/By Title		H	Displays hidden slide
Go/Slide Navigator			Moves to selected slide
Screen/Black	B		Blacks out screen
Screen/Erase	E		Erases freehand annotations
Pointer Options/Automatic			Hides slide show pointer after 15 seconds of inactivity
Pointer Options/Pen	Ctrl + P		Turns on/off freehand annotation

Screen Identification

In the following PowerPoint screen, several items are identified by letters. Enter the correct term for each item in the spaces that follow.

a. _____

b. _____

c. _____

d. _____

e. _____

f. _____

g. _____

h. _____

i. _____

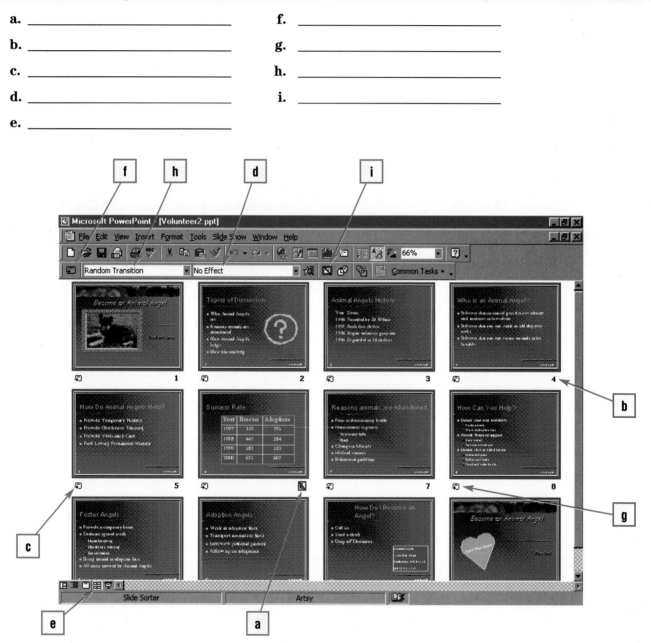

Matching

- -

Match the numbered item with the correct lettered description.

1. transitions   _____ **a.** shortcut to select all slides

2. Tools/Hide Slide   _____ **b.** used to display each bullet point, text, paragraph, or graphic independently on the slide.

3. design template   _____ **c.** special slide that controls format for the title slide only

4. slide master   _____ **d.** hides selected slide

5. builds   _____ **e.** shortcut to insert a new slide

6. [Ctrl] + A   _____ **f.** controls how one slide moves off the screen and the next one appears

7. table   _____ **g.** defines the background, text format, and placement for each slide

8. [Ctrl] + M   _____ **h.** professionally created slide designs that can be applied to a presentation

9. title master   _____ **i.** organizes information in rows and columns of cells

10. notes pages   _____ **j.** shows a miniature of the slide and provides an area to enter speaker notes

Fill-In

Complete the following statements by filling in the blanks with the correct terms.

a. _____ are professionally created slide designs that can be applied to your presentation.

b. The _____ master controls format, placement, and all elements that are to appear on every audience handout.

c. _____ refers to attributes such as bold and italics.

d. The _____ slide is a special slide on which the formatting for all slides in your presentation is defined.

e. Pressing the letter H during a presentation displays a _____ slide.

f. PowerPoint includes predefined slide layouts called _____ that are used to control the placement of objects on a slide.

g. _____ adds action to text and graphics so they move around on the screen.

h. A table is made up of _____ and _____ of cells that you can fill with text and graphics.

i. To control how one slide moves off the screen and the next one appears, you can apply _____ effects.

j. _____ are used to display each bullet point, text, paragraph, or graphic independently of the other text or objects on the slide.

Multiple Choice

Circle the letter of the correct response.

1. Selecting a _____ template changes all slides in your presentation to match the selected template design.

   a. slide

   b. design

   c. custom

   d. preview

2. A(n) _____ is a feature associated with an object or text that can be enhanced using menu commands and drawing tools.

   a. attribute

   b. font

   c. style

   d. template

3. A(n) _____ is a special slide that controls the format and placement of titles and text for all slides in a presentation.

   a. template

   b. attribute

   c. outline slide

   d. master

4. PowerPoint has _____ predefined slide layouts that can be used to control the placement of objects on a slide.

   a. 15

   b. 24

   c. 100

   d. 250

5. Slide transitions and build slides are _____ that are used to enhance the on-screen presentation.

   a. animations

   b. slide masters

   c. graphics

   d. special effects

6. Dissolve and Wipe Right are _____.

   a. builds

   b. transitions

   c. animations

   d. all of the above

7. _____ are special effects that control how a bulleted point appears to fly onto the screen.

   a. builds

   b. transitions

   c. graphics

   d. animations

8. _____ adds action to text and graphics so they move around on the screen.

   a. build

   b. transition

   c. graphic

   d. animation

9. _____ are used to define where text and graphics appear on a slide.

   a. effects

   b. placeholders

   c. slide views

   d. animations

10. To help you remember the important points, you can use speaker _____.

   a. notes pages

   b. slide handouts

   c. preview handouts

   d. handouts

True/False

Circle the correct answer to the following questions.

1. Notes pages are professionally created slide designs that can be applied to your presentation.   True   False

2. An attribute is a feature associated with a slide that can be enhanced using drawing tools and menu commands.   True   False

3. You can also apply special effects such as shadows and embossed text effects to text.   True   False

4. A master is a special slide or page on which the formatting for all slides or pages in your presentation is defined.   True   False

5. AutoLayouts are predefined slide layouts that are used to control the placement of objects on a slide.   True   False

6. A title master defines the format and placement of titles and text for slides that use the title layout.   True   False

7. A handout master defines the format and placement of the slide image, text, headers, footers, and other elements that are to appear on every onscreen presentation.   True   False

8. Builds control how one slide moves off the screen and the next one appears.   True   False

9. Transitions are used to display each bullet point, text, paragraph, or graphic independently of the other text or objects on the slide.   True   False

10. To help you remember the important points, you can use speaker notes pages.   True   False

Discussion Questions

1. Discuss how slide masters and design templates can be used to format a presentation.

2. Discuss how slide builds and transitions can be used to enhance a presentation. What should you consider before applying them to a presentation?

3. Discuss how text and object attributes can be used to make a presentation more visually appealing.

Hands-On Practice Exercises

Step by Step

Rating System ☆ Easy
☆ ☆ Moderate
☆ ☆ ☆ Difficult

☆

1. To complete this problem, you must have completed Practice Exercise 1 in Tutorial 1. Now that Jodie has learned more about how to use PowerPoint, she decides to use her newfound knowledge to further enhance the Alzheimer's presentation. Several slides of the modified presentation are shown here.

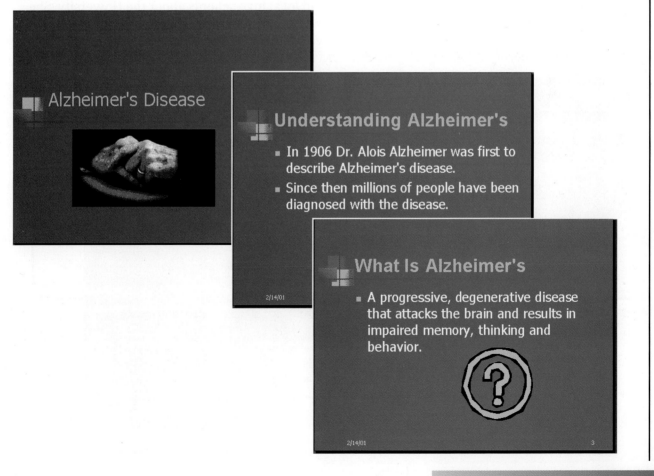

a. Open the file Alzheimer Presentation1 on your data disk.

b. Use the Find and Replace command to replace all the occurrences of "illness" with "disease."

c. Apply a new presentation design and color scheme of your choice to the presentation. Check the presentation to see how the new design has affected all slides, and move and size clip art and bulleted lists as needed.

d. Modify the text color of the titles using the title and slide masters.

e. Modify the color of the clip art on slide 3 to coordinate with the slide colors.

f. Duplicate slide 1 and place the duplicate at the end of the presentation. Replace your name with the subtitle The End.

g. Add a footer to all slides in the presentation, except the title slide, that displays the slide number and the date that will update automatically.

h. Style-check the presentation.

i. Add the Dissolve custom animation and chime sound to the clip art on slide 3.

j. Apply random transition effects to the slide show. Apply the Fly From Left build effect to slides 2, 5, 6, and 7 only.

k. Run the slide show.

l. Add file documentation and save the presentation as Alzheimer Presentation2. Print the slides as handouts (four per page).

☆

2. Bonnie is the Assistant Director of New Admissions at Arizona State University. Part of her job is to make presentations at community colleges and local high schools about the University. She has already created the introductory portion of the presentation and needs to reorganize the topics and make the presentation more visually appealing. Several slides of the modified presentation are shown here

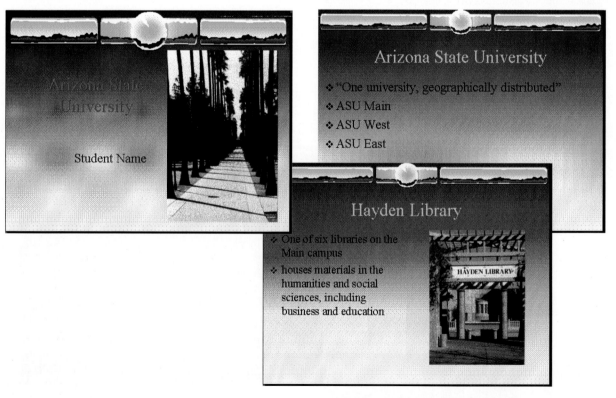

a. Open the file ASU Presentation on your data disk.

b. Run the slide show to see what Bonnie has done so far.

c. Spell-check the presentation, making the appropriate corrections.

d. Move slide 5 before slide 4.

e. Use the Find and Replace command to locate all the occurrences of "Arizona State University" and replace them with "ASU" on all slides except the first and second slides.

f. Enter your name as the subtitle in slide 1. Insert the Palm Walk picture from your data disk on the title slide. Size the picture and position the placeholders on the slide appropriately.

g. Demote all the bulleted items on slides 8 and 9 except the first item.

h. Apply a new presentation design of your choice to the presentation. Apply a new slide color scheme. Modify the text color of the titles using the title and slide masters.

i. Duplicate slide 1 and move the duplicate to the end of the presentation. Replace your name with The End.

j. Bonnie would like to add some pictures of the buildings at the end of the presentation. Switch to Slide Sorter view and select slides 12, 13, and 14. Apply the Text and Clip Art layout. Insert the Student Services picture in slide 12, the Library picture in slide 13, and the Fine Arts picture in slide 14. *Hint:* Use the Insert/Picture command to insert the picture and then drag the inserted picture into the clip art placeholder.

k. Check the style of the presentation and make any changes you feel are appropriate.

l. Add a custom animation and sound to the picture on the title slide.

m. Apply random transitions to all slides in the presentation.

n. Apply the Fly From Right build effect to all the slides with bullet items.

o. Run the slide show.

p. Add file documentation and save the presentation as ASU Presentation1. Print slides 1, 2, and 12–15 as handouts (six per page).

☆☆

3. To complete this problem, you must have completed Practice Exercise 3 in Tutorial 1. Evan, the owner of the Downtown Internet Cafe, was so impressed with your presentation on coffee that he has decided to run it periodically throughout the day on a large screen in the cafe so customers can see it as well. To "spiff it up," he wants you to convert it to an onscreen presentation with more graphics as well as other design and animation effects. Several slides of the modified presentation are shown here.

a. Open the file Coffee on your data disk.

b. Use the Replace feature to replace both instances of the term "Regular Roasts" with "Coffee Categories." Do the same to replace both instances of the term "Other Offerings" with "Coffee Types."

c. Change the design template to Sumi Painting. Select a color scheme of your choice. Check the presentation to see how the new design has affected all slides, and move and size clip art and bulleted lists as needed.

d. Change the font of the main title on the title slide to Calisto MT. Use the slide master to change the font color of all first-level bullets to a stronger color.

e. Apply a custom animation and sound of your choice to the coffee cup clip art on slide 2.

f. Change the title of slide 3 to What's Brewing?

g. Copy the clip art from slide 2 to slide 3. Delete slide 2.

h. Change the title "Central and South American Coffee" on slide 4 to Coffees from the Americas.

i. Switch to Slide Sorter view and insert a new slide with a table format after slide 7. Enter the title, Coffee Terms. Create the table with two columns and four rows. Enter What You Say as the first column heading and What It Means as the second column heading. Copy the terms and definitions from slide 9 into the table. Change the font size of the text as needed. Bold the column headings and put quotation marks around the terms. Center-align the What You Say column. Size the columns and table appropriately. Add a fill color to the table.

j. Delete slide 9.

k. Duplicate the title slide and move the duplicate to the end of the presentation. Delete the clip art. Change the title to Come have coffee with us . . . and change the subtitle text to The End. Change the font size of the subtitle to 32 pt. Move the subtitle to the lower right corner of the slide.

l. Add the following information in a text box on slide 9:

Downtown Internet Cafe
122 Main Street * Red Bank

Add a fill color and border to the text box.

m. Include your name in a footer on all slides. Hide the footer on the title slides.

n. Set the slide transition to automatically advance after 10 seconds. Run the slide show.

o. Add file documentation information and save the completed presentation as Coffee Show.

p. Print slides 1, 2, 8, and 9 as handouts, four per page.

☆☆☆

4. To complete this problem, you must have completed Practice Exercise 4 in Tutorial 1. All of the fitness trainers at Lifestyle Fitness have seen the presentation card created and attempted to relay the messages in it to their clients. But Carol has received feedback from the trainers that it would be better if the clients saw the presentation themselves. Since this presentation will now be given to the public, Carol decides that it would be more impressive as an onscreen presentation with design and animation effects than a "static" slide show. It would also be the perfect opportunity to promote the fitness programs that the center offers with a table that shows the program types and times. Several slides of the modified presentation are shown here.

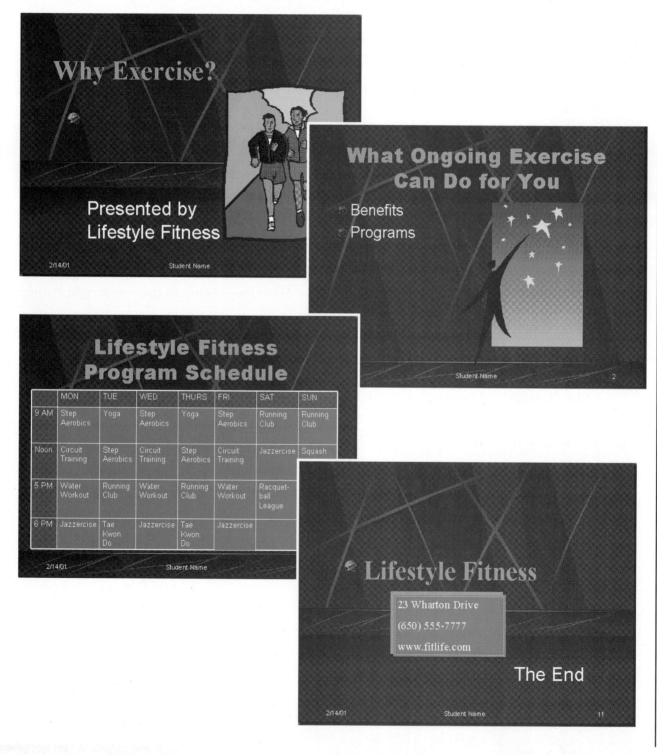

a. Open the file Exercise on your data disk. Change the design template to Network Blitz and select a color scheme of your choice.

b. Reapply the title slide layout to the title slide. Use the title master to change the main title to Times New Roman, bold, 54 pt. and the subtitle to a point size of 40. Left-align the subtitle. Reposition and move the title and subtitle and clip art appropriately.

c. Use the slide master to change the font color of the title on all slides to another color.

d. Recolor the clip art on slide 3 using colors of your choice.

e. Insert a new slide after slide 8 using the Table AutoLayout. Enter the title Lifestyle Fitness Program Schedule. Create and insert a table using the following information:

TIME	MON	TUES	WED	THURS	FRI	SAT	SUN
9 AM	Step Aerobics	Yoga	Step Aerobics	Yoga	Step Aerobics	Running Club	Running Club
Noon	Circuit Training	Step Aerobics	Circuit Training	Step Aerobics	Circuit Training	Jazzercise	Squash
5 PM	Water Workout	Running Club	Water Workout	Running Club	Water Workout	Racquetball League	Racquetball League
6 PM	Jazzercise	Tae Kwon Do	Jazzercise	Tae Kwon Do	Jazzercise		

f. Change the font size of the table text to 16 pt. and adjust the column width and row height. Add fill colors to the headings and events boxes as you like.

g. Insert a new title slide at the end of the presentation Enter Lifestyle Fitness as the title and The End as the subtitle. Add the following text in a text box:

23 Wharton Drive
(602) 555-7777
www.fitlife.com

h. Size the text box appropriately and add a color fill and border. Apply a shadow effect to the text box. Reposition the title, subtitle, and text box appropriately.

i. Add the following note to slide 10 using a font size of 20:

Fat analysis done upon request. Ask at front desk.
Personal trainers available Monday through Friday from 10–5.
Special fitness workshops offered periodically. Check calendar in lobby.

j. Hide the footer on the title slides.

k. Add transition and build effects of your choice to all slides except slides 1 and 11. Run the slide show.

l. Check the presentation style and make changes as appropriate.

m. Add file documentation and save the completed presentation as Exercise for Clients. Print the handouts (three per page) for all slides and the notes page for slide 10.

☆☆☆

5. To complete this problem, you must have completed Practice Exercise 5 in Tutorial 1. You showed your first draft of the presentation about the market analysis for The Sports Company to the marketing manager. Damon has some additional information he wants you to add to the presentation. Additionally, he wants you to make the presentation look better using many of the PowerPoint design and slide show presentation features. Several slides of the modified presentation are shown here.

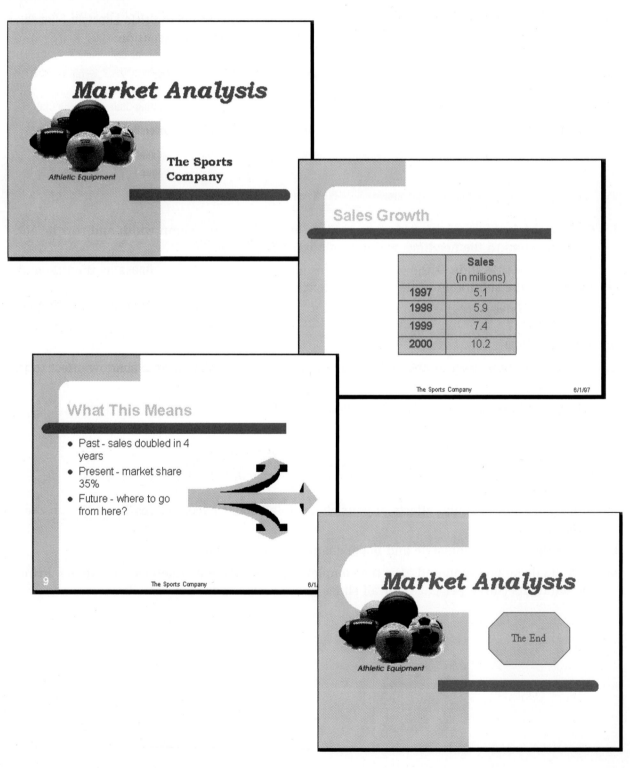

a. Open the file Marketing Presentation on your data disk. If necessary, switch to Normal view.

b. Change the design template to Capsules. Reapply the title layout to the title slide. Change the color scheme to yellow with a custom color of your choice for the Text and Lines and Title options.

c. Change the font of the title on the title master to Bookman Old Style or similar font. Change the font size to 54 pt. Apply italics and a shadow to the title line. Change the text color of the subtitle to a color of your choice, bold it, and change it to the same font as the title.

d. Apply the layout Text and Clip Art to slide 8. Insert the clip art Arrows from your data disk into the slide. Drag it into the clip art placeholder. Modify the clip art color to match the text color. Add a custom animation and sound to the clip art.

e. Insert a new slide after slide 4 using the Table layout. Enter the title Sales Growth. Create a two column by five-row table. Enter the following data in the table.

	Sales (in millions)
1997	5.1
1998	5.9
1999	7.4
2000	10.2

f. Format the table by sizing the columns, applying border colors, and bolding and centering the data in the table.

g. Switch to Slide Sorter view and hide slide 4.

h. Duplicate the title slide and move it to the end of the presentation. Delete the subtitle placeholder. Add a drawing object to this slide that includes the text The End.

i. Hide the footer on the title slides.

j. Add transition and build effects of your choice to all the slides except slide 2. Run the slide show.

k. Add the following note to slide 3 in a point size of 20.

The next slide displays the same information in a table. It is hidden.

l. Style-check the presentation and make any changes necessary.

m. Add file documentation and save the completed presentation as Final Marketing Presentation.

n. Print the notes page for slide 3, and print slides 1, 2, 5, 9, and 10 as handouts with three slides per page.

On Your Own

☆

6.   You work at an employment agency and your manager has asked you to create an onscreen presentation about interview techniques. This presentation will be loaded on all the computers that your company makes available to clients for online job searches, and instructions on how to run the presentation will be posted at each workstation. Select a presentation design that you like and create the presentation using the following notes for reference. Add clip art and build effects where applicable. Add your name to a footer on each slide except the title slide. Set the slide transition so that it automatically advances after an appropriate length of time (long enough for the person viewing the presentation to read each slide's contents).

Before a job interview, you should thoroughly research the company (use the library or the Web). For example, what is one event that occurred in the company within the last five years?

During the interview, demonstrate your expertise, using a consultant's style of communicating. Create open and clear communication, and effectively respond to open-ended questions. Examples of open-ended questions are: "Tell me about yourself." "What makes you stand out?" "What are your greatest weaknesses?" You should also be ready to answer questions about why you are interviewing with the company and how and where you fit within their organization. You must be prepared to handle both spoken and unspoken objections. And finally, you must justify your salary requirements, don't just negotiate them.

☆☆

7.   To finish creating the basic Better Bikes Company presentation on cycling tips that you began in Tutorial 1, Practice Exercise 6, you need to turn it into an onscreen presentation with a custom design, clip art, sound, transitions, and builds so it will hold your audience's interest. You also need to add speaker notes and rehearse the presentation before giving it to the school PTA. When you are done, save and print the presentation as handouts and print the notes pages for slides containing notes only.

☆☆

8.   To complete the presentation on family financial planning that you began in the On Your Own exercise 8 in Tutorial 1, you want to add a simple table that shows typical money allocations for a middle-income family and customize the design. Open the presentation and apply and customize a new design template. Insert a slide with a table that shows sample monthly incomes and budget allocations (for rent/house payments, utilities, food, clothing, entertainment, etc.). Enhance the table appropriately. Add clip art, animation, transitions, and builds where appropriate. Add speaker notes to at least two slides with explanatory information or personal anecdotes relating to those slides. Save the presentation. Print the notes pages for the slides containing speaker notes. Print handouts (6 per page) for the entire presentation.

9.   After completing the Web design presentation in Tutorial 1, exercise 9, you decide it needs a bit more sprucing up. First of all, it would be more impressive as an onscreen presentation with a custom design. Also, the pros and cons information would look better as a table, and a few animated clip art pictures, non-standard bullets, builds, and transitions wouldn't hurt. Make these and any other changes that you think would enhance the presentation. When you are done, save and print the presentation as handouts and the notes pages for slides containing notes only.

10.   You and your fellow Getaway Travel Club members have decided that each of you should do a presentation on your favorite vacation spot (one you've already been to or one you'd like to go to). Pick a location and do some research on the Web and/or visit a local travel agency to get information about your chosen destination. Create a presentation using a custom design and include clip art, animation, sounds, transitions, and build effects to make the presentation more interesting. Include your name as a footer or subtitle on at least one slide. Use speaker notes if necessary to remind yourself of additional information you want to relay that is not included in the slides. Run the slide show and practice your presentation, then save and print your presentation and notes pages.

Working Together: Copying and Linking Between Word, Excel, and PowerPoint

Case Study   The agency director of Animal Angels has reviewed the PowerPoint presentation you created and has asked you to include a chart created in Excel showing the adoption success rate. Additionally, the director has provided a list of dates for the upcoming volunteer orientation meetings that she feels would be good content for another slide.

Frequently you will find that you will want to include information that was created using a word processor, spreadsheet, or database application in your slide show. As you will see, it is easy to share information between applications, saving you both time and effort by eliminating the need to recreate information that is available in another application. You will learn how to share information between applications while you create the new slides. The new slides containing information from Word and Excel are shown here.

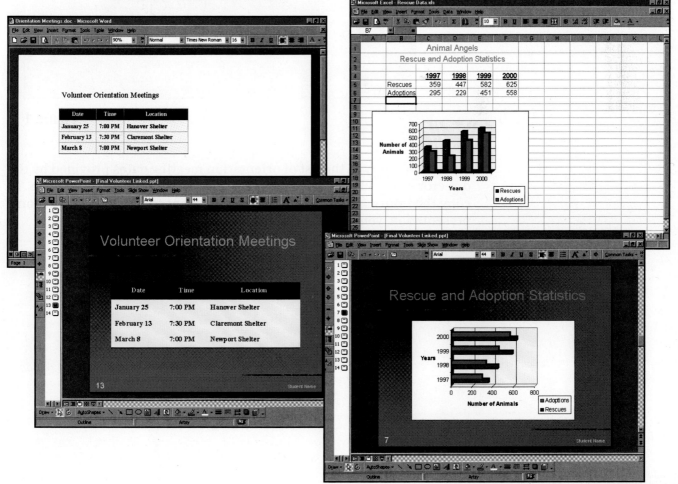

Note: The Working Together section assumes that you already know how to use Word and Excel 2000 and that you have completed Tutorial 2 of PowerPoint. You will need the file Final Volunteer you saved at the end of Tutorial 2 of PowerPoint.

Copying Between Applications

First you will modify the PowerPoint presentation to include the orientation meeting dates.

1 Start PowerPoint.

■ Open the file Final Volunteer.

■ Insert a new slide in the Title Only AutoLayout after slide 11.

■ Display the new slide in Slide view.

Your screen should be similar to Figure 1.

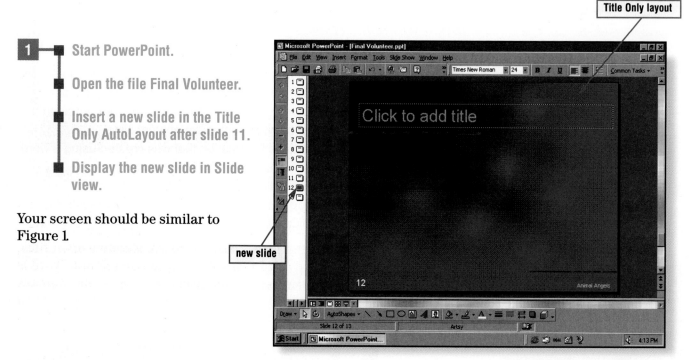

Figure 1

Rather than retype the list of orientation meeting dates provided by the director, you will copy it from the Word document into the new slide. To copy the information from the Word document file into the PowerPoint presentation, you need to open the Word document.

2 ■ Start Word 2000.

■ Open the file Orientation Meetings.

Use the Start button or display the desktop and click

Your screen should be similar to Figure 2.

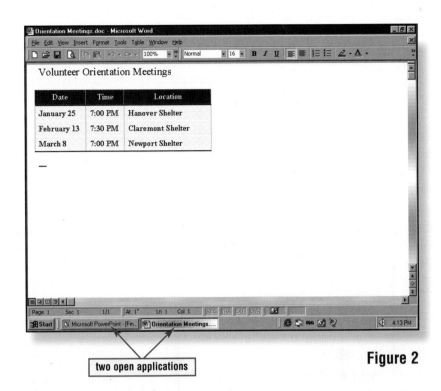

two open applications

Figure 2

There are now two open applications, Word and PowerPoint. PowerPoint is open in a window behind the Word application window. Both application buttons are displayed in the taskbar. There are also two open files, Orientation Meetings in Word and Final Volunteer in PowerPoint. Word is the active application, and Orientation Meetings is the active file. To make it easier to work with two applications, you will tile the windows to view both on the screen at the same time.

3 ■ Right-click on a blank area of the taskbar to open the shortcut menu.

■ Select Tile Windows Vertically.

■ Click on the Word document window to make it active.

Your screen should be similar to Figure 3.

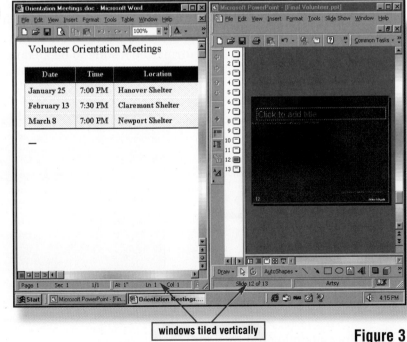

windows tiled vertically

Figure 3

First you will copy the title from the Word document into the title of the slide. While using the Word and PowerPoint applications, you have learned how to use cut, copy, and paste to move or copy information within the same document. You can also perform these same operations between documents in the same application and between documents in different applications. The information is pasted in a format that the application can edit, if possible.

4 ■ Select the title (excluding the blank space at the end of the title).

■ Drag the selection using the right mouse button to the title placeholder in the slide.

> If you drag using the left mouse button the selection is moved.

■ From the shortcut menu, select Copy Here.

> You could also use Copy and Paste to copy the title to the slide.

■ Clear the selection.

Your screen should be similar to Figure 4.

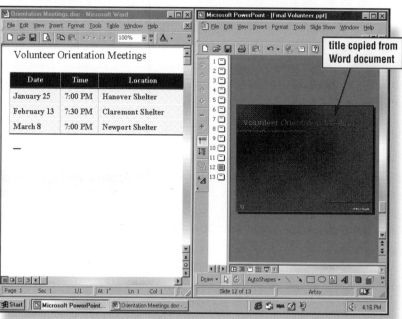

Figure 4

The title has been copied into the slide and can be edited and manipulated within PowerPoint. The formats associated with the slide master are applied to the copied text. If the copied text included formatting, such as color, it would override the slide master settings, just as if you individually formatted a slide to make it unique. Next you want to display the table of orientation dates below the title in the slide.

5 ■ Select the table in the Word document window.

> Drag to select the entire table or use Table/Select/Table.

■ Click 📋.

■ Click on the PowerPoint window.

■ Choose Edit/Paste Special.

The Paste Special dialog box on your screen should be similar to Figure 5.

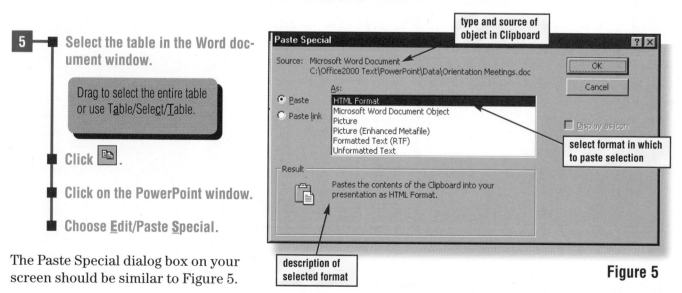

Figure 5

The Paste Special dialog box displays the type of object contained in the Clipboard and its location in the Source area. From the As list box, you select the type of format in which you want the object inserted into the destination file. The default option inserts the copy in HTML (HyperText Markup Language) format. The Result area describes the effect of your selections. In this case, you want the object inserted as a picture.

6 ■ **From the As list box, select Picture.**

■ **Click** `OK` **.**

Your screen should be similar to Figure 6.

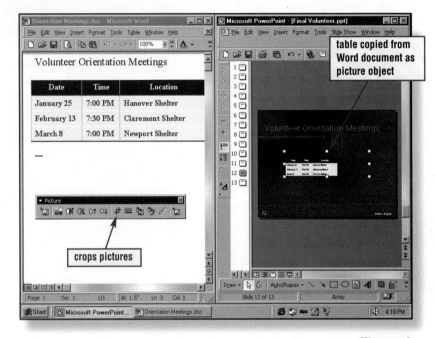

Figure 6

The table, including the table formatting, is copied into the slide. The picture object can be manipulated using the Picture toolbar. You will trim or crop the object so that the object size is the same size as the table. Then you will increase the size of the object and position it in the slide.

7 Choose Undo Tile from the Taskbar shortcut menu.

If necessary, maximize the PowerPoint window.

Click 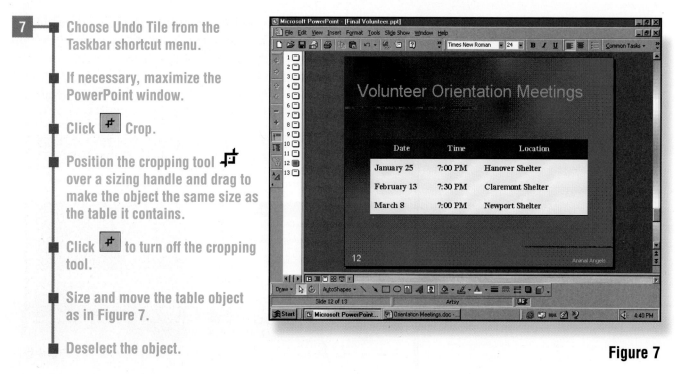 Crop.

Position the cropping tool over a sizing handle and drag to make the object the same size as the table it contains.

Click to turn off the cropping tool.

Size and move the table object as in Figure 7.

Deselect the object.

Figure 7

Your screen should be similar to Figure 7.

8 Click  in the taskbar to switch to the Word application.

Exit Word.

Linking an Excel Chart to a PowerPoint Presentation

Next you are going to insert the chart of the rescue and adoption data into another new slide. This slide will follow slide 6.

1 Insert a new slide using the
Title Only AutoLayout following
slide 6.

Display the new slide in Slide
view.

Load Excel 2000 and open the
file Rescue Data on your data
disk.

Tile the application windows
vertically.

Your screen should be similar to
Figure 8.

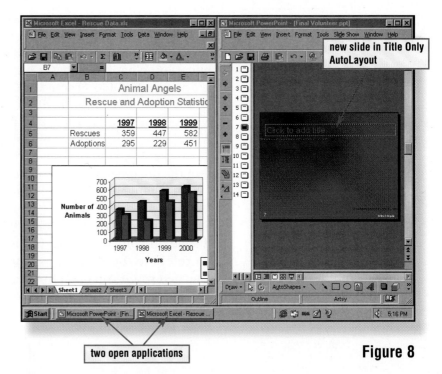

Figure 8

The worksheet contains the rescue and adoption data for the past four
years and a column chart of the data. Again, you have two open applications, PowerPoint and Excel. Next you will copy the second title line from
the worksheet into the slide title placeholder.

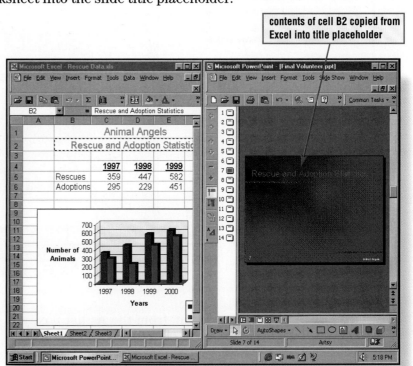

2 Select cell B2.

Copy the selection to the Title
placeholder in the slide.

Remove the extra blank line
below the title.

Size the placeholder and position
the title appropriately on the
slide.

Clear the selection.

Your screen should be similar to
Figure 9.

Figure 9

Next you will copy the chart into the slide. You will insert the chart object into the slide as a **linked object**. Information created in one application can also be inserted as a linked object into a document created by another application. When an object is linked, the data is stored in the **source file** (the document it was created in). A graphic representation or picture of the data is displayed in the **destination file** (the document in which the object is inserted). A connection between the information in the destination file to the source file is established by the creation of a link. The link contains references to the location of the source file and the selection within the document that is linked to the destination file.

When changes are made in the source file that affect the linked object, the changes are automatically reflected in the destination file when it is opened. This is called a **live link**. When you create linked objects, the date and time on your machine should be accurate. This is because the program refers to the date of the source file to determine whether updates are needed when you open the destination file.

By making the chart a linked object, it will be automatically updated if the source file is edited. To create a linked object,

3 ■ Select the chart.

  Click on the chart to select it when the Screentip displays Chart Area.

■ Click 🗎 Copy.

■ Click on the slide.

■ Choose Edit/Paste Special.

■ Select Paste Link.

Your screen should be similar to Figure 10.

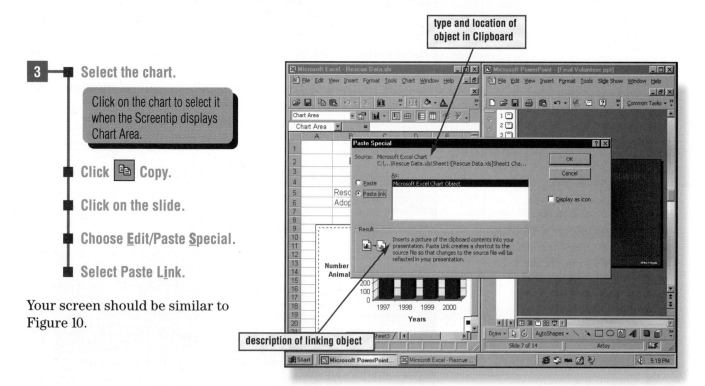

Figure 10

Again, from the As list box, you select the type of format in which you want the object inserted into the destination file. The only available option for this object is as a Microsoft Excel Chart Object. The Result area describes the effect of your selections. In this case, the object will be inserted as a picture, and a link will be created to the chart in the source file. Selecting the Display as Icon option changes the display of the object from a picture to an icon. Double-clicking the icon displays the object picture. The default selections are appropriate.

4 ■ Click [OK].

■ Appropriately size and center the linked object on the slide.

■ Deselect the object.

Your screen should be similar to Figure 11.

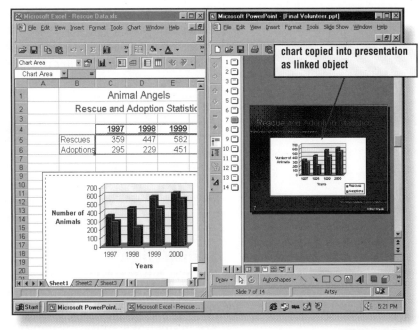

Figure 11

While looking at the chart in the slide, you decide to change the chart type from a column chart to a bar chart. You feel a bar chart will show the trends more clearly. You also notice the Adoption data for 1998 looks very low. After checking the original information you see you entered the wrong value in the worksheet and need to correct the value to 329.

To make these changes, you need to switch back to Excel. Double-clicking on a linked object quickly switches to the open source file. If the source file is not open, it opens the file for you. If the application is not loaded, it both loads the application and opens the source file.

The menu equivalent is Edit/Linked Object/Open.

5 ■ Double-click the chart object in the slide.

■ Click ■ Chart Type.

■ Select 3-D Bar Chart.

■ Edit the value in cell D6 to **329**.

Your screen should be similar to Figure 12.

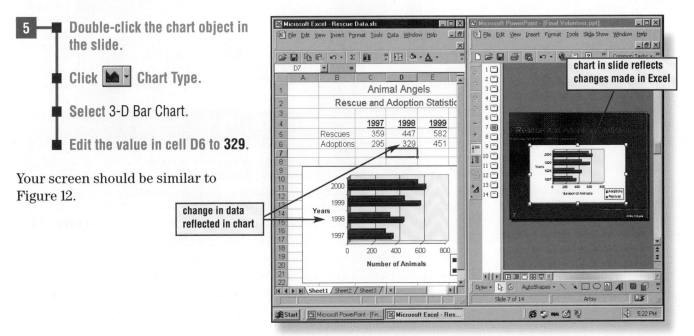

Figure 12

The chart type in both applications has changed to a bar chart, and the chart data series has been updated to reflect the change in data. This is because any changes you make in the chart in Excel will be automatically reflected in the linked chart in the slide.

6 ■ Untile the application windows.

■ Save the revised worksheet file as Rescue Data Linked.

■ Exit Excel.

■ If necessary, maximize the PowerPoint window.

Editing Links

Whenever a document is opened that contains links, the application looks for the source file and automatically updates the linked objects. If there are many links, updating can take a lot of time. Additionally, if you move the source file to another location, or perform other operations that may interfere with the link, your link will not work. To help with situations like these, you can edit the settings associated with links. To see how you do this,

1 ■ If necessary, select the chart object.

■ Choose Edit/Links.

Your screen should be similar to Figure 13.

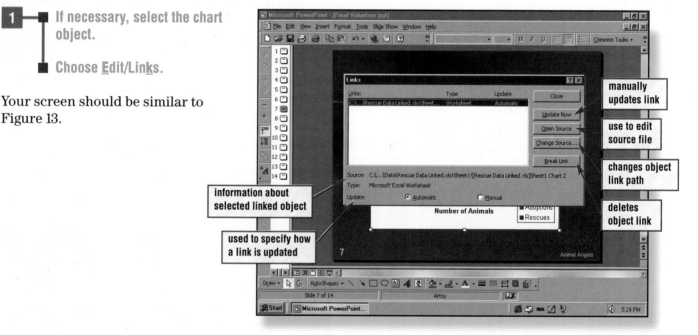

Figure 13

The Links dialog box displays the object path for all links in the document in the list box. The field code specifies the path and name of the source file, the range of linked cells or object name, the type of file, and the update status. Below the list box the details for the selected link are displayed. The other options in this dialog box are described in the table below.

Option	Effect
Automatic	Updates the linked object whenever the destination document is opened or the source file changes. This is the default.
Manual	The destination document is not automatically updated and you must use the Update Now command button to update the link.
Locked	Prevents a linked object from being updated.
Open Source	Opens the source document for the selected link
Change Source	Used to modify the path to the source document.
Break Link	Breaks the connection between the source document and the active document

You do not want to make any changes to the link.

2 ■ Click Close .

Linking documents is a very handy feature, particularly in documents whose information is updated frequently. If you include a linked object in a document that you are giving to another person, make sure the user has access to the source file and application. Otherwise the links will not operate correctly.

Next you will print the two new slides.

Use  to apply the footer to the selected slides only.

3 ■ Use **View/Header** and Footer to modify the slide footer to display your name on slides 7 and 13 only.

■ Choose **File/Print**.

■ Specify slides 7 and 13 as the slides to print in the Slides text box.

■ Select Handouts as the output with two slides per page.

■ Print the slides.

■ Save the PowerPoint presentation as **Final Volunteer Linked** and exit PowerPoint.

Key Terms

destination file   PPW-5
linked object   PPW-8
live link   PPW-8
source file   PPW-8

Command Summary

Command	Action
Edit/Paste Special/Picture	Inserts a selection as a picture object
Edit/Paste Special/Paste Link	Inserts a selection as a linked object
Edit/Links	Changes settings associated with linked objects
Edit/Linked Object/Open	Opens the source application of the linked object

Hands-On Practice Exercises

Step by Step

1 To complete this problem, you must have completed Practice Exercise 1 in Tutorial 2. The Alzheimer's presentation is almost complete. Jodie just needs to add some information to the presentation about the progression of Alzheimers. This information is already in a Word document, so Jodie just wants to copy it into a new slide.

a. Load Word and open the Alzheimer Scale file on your data disk.

b. Load PowerPoint and open the Alzheimer Presentation2 file on your data disk.

c. Add a new slide after slide 7 using the Title Only layout.

d. Copy the title from the Word document into the slide title placeholder.

e. Copy the table of stages of Alzheimer's into the slide as a picture object.

f. Size and position it appropriately.

g. Save the presentation as Alzheimer Presentation3.

h. Add your name as a footer to this slide only.

i. Print the new slide.

Scale for Stages of Alzheimer's

Scale	Stage	Characteristics
1	Normal Adult	No functional decline.
2	Normal Older Adult	Personal awareness of some functional decline.
3	Early Alzheimer's	Noticeable deficits in demanding job situations.
4	Mild Alzheimer's	Requires assistance in complicated tasks such as handling finances, planning parties, etc.
5	Moderate Alzheimer's	Requires assistance in choosing proper attire.
6	Moderately Severe Alzheimer's	Requires assistance dressing, bathing, and toileting. Experiences urinary and fecal incontinence.
7	Severe Alzheimer's	Speech ability declines to about a half-dozen intelligible words. Progressive loss of abilities to walk, sit up, smile, and hold head up.

2/15/01 Student Name 8

☆☆

2. To complete this problem, you must have completed Practice Exercise 3 in Tutorial 2. Evan, owner of the Downtown Internet Cafe, wants you to include information about special prices on coffee beans in the coffee slide show you created. You will link the coffee price information to the presentation because the prices change frequently with market conditions and good buys.

a. Load Word and open the document Coffee Prices on your data disk.

b. Load PowerPoint and open the presentation Coffee Show.

c. Add a new slide at the end of the presentation using the Title Only layout.

d. Enter the slide title ... Or Take Some Home.

e. Copy the table of prices into the slide as a linked object. Size and position the object appropriately.

f. In the Word document, change the price of the Kenyan blend to $9.95.

g. Save the Word document as Coffee Prices Linked. Exit Word.

...Or Take Some Home

Coffee	Description	Cost/Pound
Columbian Blend	Classic body and aroma	$8.50
French Roast	Sophisticated taste	$9.25
Kenyan	Robust and deep flavor	$9.95
Arabian Blend	Strong yet subtle	$7.95

2/15/01 Student Name 10

> **h.** Add your name as a footer to this slide only.
>
> **i.** Save the PowerPoint presentation as Coffee Show Linked.
>
> **j.** Print the new slide.

☆ ☆ ☆

3. To complete this problem, you must have completed Practice Exercise 4 of Tutorial 2. Carol Hayes, program coordinator for Lifestyle Fitness, has found some interesting data about fitness trends over the past 10 years. She wants to include this information in a presentation she has created for clients.

> **a.** Load PowerPoint and open the Exercise for Clients presentation.
>
> **b.** Load Excel and open the Fitness Activity worksheet on your data disk.
>
> **c.** Add two new slides after slide 10 using the Title Only layout.
>
> **d.** Copy the title from cell B3 into the title placeholder for slide 11. Size and position it appropriately.
>
> **e.** Copy the worksheet range B5 through E10 as a linked object into slide 11. Size and position it appropriately.
>
> **f.** Copy the title from cell B14 into the title placeholder for slide 12. Size and position it appropriately.
>
> **g.** Copy the chart into slide 12 as a linked object. Size and position it appropriately.
>
> **h.** You notice that the percentage for use of a treadmill seems low. After checking the original source, you see you mistakenly entered the value for 1993 as the 1997 value. Change the value in cell E9 to **36.1**. Treadmill use has increased from 16 percent to 26 percent.
>
> **i.** Save the worksheet as Fitness Activity Linked. Exit Excel.
>
> **j.** Add your name as a footer to this slide only.
>
> **k.** Print the new slide.
>
> **l.** Save the presentation as Exercise Linked.

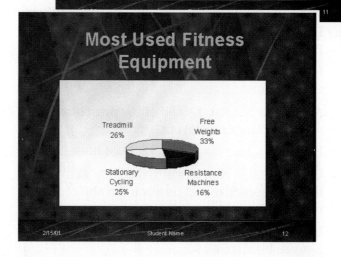

Glossary of Key Terms

Alignment: Settings that allow you to change the horizontal placement of an entry in a placeholder or a table cell.

Attribute: A feature associated with an object or text that can be enhanced using drawing tools and menu commands.

AutoContent Wizard: A guided approach that helps you determine the content and organization of your presentation through a series of questions.

AutoCorrect: A feature that makes basic assumptions about the text you are typing and automatically corrects the entry.

AutoLayout: Ready-made shapes, such as circles and stars, that are supplied with Office 2000.

AutoShapes: A predefined slide layout that is used to control the placement of elements on a slide.

Build: An effect that progressively displays the bulleted items as the presentation proceeds.

Clip art: A collection of simple line art drawings that is usually bundled with a software program.

Custom dictionary: A dictionary you can create to hold words you commonly use but that are not included in the dictionary that is supplied with the program.

Demote: To move a topic down one level in the outline hierarchy.

Design template: Professionally created slide design that can be applied to your presentation.

Destination file: The document receiving a linked object.

Drawing object: An object consisting of shapes such as lines and boxes that can be created using the Drawing toolbar.

Drawing toolbar: A toolbar that is used to add objects such as lines, circles, and boxes.

Font size: Height of a character measured in points.

Font: A set of characters with a specific design.

Footer: Text or graphics that appear on the bottom of each slide.

Formatting toolbar: A toolbar that contains buttons used to modify text.

Graphics: Non-text elements, such as charts, drawings, pictures, and scanned photographs, in a slide.

Linked object: An object that is created in a source file and linked to a destination file. Edits made to the source file are automatically reflected in the destination file.

Live link: A link that automatically updates the linked object whenever changes are made to it in the source file.

Main dictionary: Dictionary that comes with the PowerPoint 2000 program.

Master: A special slide on which the formatting of all slides in a presentation is defined.

Move handle: Used to move menu bars and toolbars to a new location.

Notes page: Printed output that shows a miniature of the slide and provides an area for speaker notes.

Object: An item on a slide that can be selected and modified.

Office Assistant: Used to get help on features specific to the Office application you are using.

Outlining toolbar: Displayed in Outline view, it is used to modify the presentation outline.

Pane: In Normal view, the separate divisions of the window that allow you to work on all aspects of your presentation in one place.

Picture: An illustration created by combining lines, arcs, circles, and other shapes.

Placeholder: A box that is designed to contain objects such as the slide title, bulleted text, charts, tables, and pictures.

Point: A unit of type measurement. One point equals about 1/72 inch.

Promote: To move a topic up one level in the outline hierarchy.

Rotate handle: A handle that allows you to rotate the selected object to any degree in any direction.

Sans serif font: A font, such as Arial or Helvetica, that does not have a flair at the base of each letter.

Selection handle: See sizing handle.

Selection rectangle: Hashed border surrounding a selected placeholder.

Serif font: A font, such as Bookman or Times New Roman, that has a flair at the base of each letter.

Sizing handles: Small boxes surrounding selected objects that are used to change the size of the object.

Slide show: An onscreen display of a presentation as the audience would see it.

Slide: An individual page of the presentation.

Source file: The document in which a linked object is created.

Standard toolbar: A toolbar that contains buttons that give quick access to the most frequently used program features.

Style: Refers to the attributes, such as bold and italics, that can be applied to text.

Tab stop: A stopping point along a line to which text will indent when you press Tab.

Transition: An effect that controls how a slide moves off the screen and the next one appears.

View: A way of looking at the presentation. Five views are available in PowerPoint.

Workspace: Large area of the application window where the presentation is displayed.

Command Summary

Command	Shortcut	Button	Action
File/New	Ctrl + N		Creates new presentation
File/Open	Ctrl + O		Opens selected presentation
File/Close			Closes presentation
File/Save	Ctrl + S		Saves presentation
File/Save As			Saves presentation using new file name
File/Print	Ctrl + P		Prints presentation using default print settings
File/Properties			Displays statistics and enters information about the file
File/Exit			Exits PowerPoint program
Edit/Undo	Ctrl + Z		Erases the last action
Edit/Paste Special/Picture			Inserts a selection as a picture object
Edit/Paste Special/Paste Link			Inserts a selection as a linked object
Edit/Select All	Ctrl + A		Selects all slides in presentation, all text and graphics in active window, or all text in a selected object
Edit/Delete Slide	Delete		Deletes selected slide
Edit/Find	Ctrl + F		Finds selected text
Edit/Replace	Ctrl + H		Replaces selected text
Edit/Links			Changes settings associated with linked objects
View/Normal			Switches to Normal view
View/Notes Page			Displays notes pages
View/Slide Sorter			Switches to Slide Sorter view
View/Slide Show	F5		Runs slide show
View/Master/Slide Master	⇧ Shift + ▭		Displays slide master for current presentation
View/Master/Title Master			Displays title master for current presentation

Command	Shortcut Key	Button	Action
View/Black and White			Displays slides in black and white
View/Slide Miniature			Displays or hides miniature version of slides
View/Ruler			Turns on/off display of ruler
View/Header and Footer			Specifies information that appears as headers and footers on slides, notes, outlines, and handout pages
Insert/New Slide	Ctrl + M		Inserts new slide
Insert/Duplicate Slide			Inserts duplicate of selected slide
Insert/Picture/Clip Art			Opens ClipArt Gallery and inserts selected clip art
Insert/Text Box			Adds a text box
Insert/Picture/AutoShapes			Inserts an AutoShape object
Insert/Picture/From File			Inserts a picture from file on disk
Format/Font/Font		Arial Narrow	Changes font type
Format/Font/Size		24	Changes font size
Format/Font/Font Style/Bold		B	Changes font type
Format/Alignment/Align Left	Ctrl + L		Left aligns selection
Format/Alignment/Center	Ctrl + E		Center aligns selection
Format/Alignment/Align Right	Ctrl + R		Right aligns selection
Format/Alignment/Justify			Justifies selection
Format/Font/Font/Color		A	Adds color to selection
Format/Slide Layout			Changes or creates a slide layout
Format/Slide Color Scheme			Changes color scheme of one or all slides in a presentation
Format/Background			Changes color of slide background
Format/Apply Design Template			Changes appearance of slide by applying a different design template
Format/Picture/Recolor			Sets color and style option
Tools/Spelling	F7		Spell-checks presentation
Tools/Options/Spelling and Style			Sets spelling and style options
Slide Show/Preset Animation		No Effect	Adds builds to selected slides
Slide Show/Slide Transition			Adds transition effects
Slide Show /Hide Slide			Hides selected slide

Command	Shortcut Key	Button	Action
Slide Show Shortcut Menu			
Go/By Title		[H]	Displays hidden slide
Go/Slide Navigator			Moves to a specific slide
Screen/Black		[B]	Blacks out screen
Screen/Erase		[E]	Erases freehand annotations
Pointer Options/Automatic			Sets pointer to an arrow and hides after 15 seconds of nonuse
Pointer Options/Pen	Ctrl + P		Turns on/off freehand annotation

Index

Notes